The ABC's
of Islamism

*Everything you wanted to know about
radical islam but where afraid to ask*

By Raheel Raza

The ABC's of Islamism, by Raheel Raza

ISBN Print - 978-1-7771986-2-6

ISBN Ebook - 978-1-7771986-4-0

ISBN Audio - 978-1-7771986-3-3

About Rebel News

Rebel News is a leading independent source of news, opinion and activism. Launched by Ezra Levant and a group of dedicated Rebels after the Sun News Network shut down, Rebel News's motto is "telling the other side of the story" — in Canada and across the world.

For more information about Rebel News, or more copies of this book, please visit *www.RebelNews.com*

"Raheel Raza notes early in her excellent *A to Z of Islamism* that 'Islam is a faith like Judaism and Christianity. Islamism is a political ideology' like fascism and communism. This insight underlies her humane, elegant, and powerful analysis of the utopian movement she had fled her native Pakistan to escape - and now is dismayed to find in her adopted country of Canada. May her clarion voice, along with an ever-growing cohort of anti-Islamist Muslims, help us in the West to defeat a hideous phenomenon."

Daniel Pipes, Middle East Forum

I was, sadly, very pleased and relieved to read this very important new book by Raheel Raza. Sad, because it exposes so many evidence-based highly significant descriptions of deeply disturbing developments in Canada. Relieved, because these developments need to be known, understood and to generate appropriate responses

I and many colleagues are profoundly concerned about the expansion of the Islamist ideology and associated practices here in our own country - and in many other countries, such as Nigeria, where Islamist militias have been (and still are) massacring thousands of Christians and Muslims who do not adopt the Islamist ideology.

It is therefore imperative that we who wish to preserve the fundamental values of democracy, including freedom of belief and freedom of speech, become aware of the dangers associated with the development of Islamism and develop policies to protect our political, cultural and spiritual heritage.

The Baroness Caroline Cox, British House of Lords

Contents

Preface

For over two thousand years, three Abrahamic religions have determined the course of history for a great swath of humanity. Frequent interchanges between and amongst them have been forbearing at best, horribly bloody at worst.

But until the Holocaust, there was no formal process resembling what we now take for granted as "interfaith" dialogue. Since the mid-twentieth century, dialogue between Jews and Christians has evolved from hesitant outreach to acknowledgement of avoidable past tragedies, thence to reconciliation and mutual respect.

But between Muslims and Christians, and between Muslims and Jews, the necessary trust and good will for rapprochement involving complete transparency of the kind governing Christian-Jewish dialogue has been harder to come by. The modern resurgence of political Islam — Islamism, a totalitarian ideology that wears the mask of religion — is the elephant blocking any meaningful dialogue's conference room door.

Interfaith dialogue is a western custom, a byproduct of democracy, religious pluralism and the Judeo-Christian tradition of objective internal performance review. Historically, Islam has not treated its internal performance reviewers kindly. A number of secular Muslims willingly denounce Islamism. But they are in turn denounced by defensive activists who insist Islam is only, and has ever been, a religion of peace, and that criticism of Islamism is the thin edge of Islamophobia

– a charged term that is itself hotly contested in the West, and for good reason.

All this to say that pious, deeply-informed Muslims of an ecumenical bent, blessed with natural leadership, high intelligence and exquisite diplomatic skills, committed to democratic principles, and eager to join forces formally with non-Muslims – Christians, Jews, Hindus and atheists, whoever — in open condemnation of Islamism, while at the same time defending the virtues of enlightened Islam, do not, shall we say, grow on trees in Canada.

Raheel Raza, my model for the paragraph above, boasts other important attributes: an indomitable sense of mission backed by steely courage, softened by a wicked sense of humour, boundless warmth and the patience of Job. Raheel, her family and a small idealistic circle of like-minded Muslims and their allies plow their outreach furrow via the Council of Muslims Facing Tomorrow. As well, Raheel promotes her vision through journalism, her award-winning documentary film *Honor Diaries*, which exposed gender inequality and gender iniquities in Muslim-majority societies, and through countless appearances at hearings and conferences all over the world.

In her slim new book, *ABC's of Islamism*, Raheel has amassed an informative, reader-friendly compendium of her many columns over recent years on Islamism, columns which address the thorniest nettles in Islam's tangled garden, grasping every one with hands callused by a lifetime of experience in separating blossoms from weeds.

For example, under Anti-Semitism, she flatly states, in contradiction to the widely-believed assumption that Islam is inherently anti-Semitic: "Anti-Semitism has a direct connection with the rise of Islamism. Islamism is based on an ideology of hate and dehumanization so the Islamists have singled out Jews and Israel as their common enemy. Much of this is fanned by the Middle East crisis…"

Coincident with this book's publication, we are witnessing the astonishing breakup of the Middle East logjam, with Israel and neighbouring Arab states having signed the Abraham Accord, a validation of Raheel's claim, and a stunning rebuke to the received wisdom that their religion would never allow Arabs to make common cause with Jews.

She argues under "Gender Jihad" that it is not Islam per se that forces women into burqas, turning them into "submissive stacks of laundry with legs we too frequently see represented in the media." It is a combination of tribalism and Islamism. Under Islam proper, women had inheritance rights, the right to abortion and birth control, and a history , long forgotten, of powerful roles in business and politics.

As one of the few journalists in Canada that supports a ban on the niqab in public-service roles, I am gratified to see a Muslim authority take a similar public stand. In the present moment of obsession with anything that even superficially smacks of discrimination against the Other, one needs to be rhetorically nimble in countering such accusations whenever the issue of face cover arises. Raheel proves that face cover is only coincidentally tied to Islam and makes a solid case for discouraging its use in public.

Under "Islamism," Raheel delivers a short, succinct and informative history of previous waves of this pernicious ideology. Islamism comes in violent and soft varieties. Canada has been heavily infiltrated by what is sometimes referred to as the "stealth jihad." Raheel's introduction details the variety of ways in which an anti-western, self-serving brand of political Islam has infiltrated Canada's institutions, citing, as a troubling example of Canadian politicians' intoxication with multiculturalism and the pleasure of virtue-signaling, the near-success of a 2004 push for Shariah law's official status in Ontario. Her scathing indictment of Motion 103, an attempt by soft jihadists to forestall criticism of Islam through a blasphemy law in everything but name, is by itself reason enough to acquire this book.

Raheel Raza should be hailed as a national treasure. Instead, she receives literal fatwas from Islamists, which she often jokes about, but which in reality are no laughing matter, and awkward silence from confused Canadians who take their cue from official Islamism-apologist Muslim associations. Politicians shun her – not because they are confused, but because they have no honour, and know who is best placed to deliver Muslim votes.

Kol ha kovod – in Hebrew this means "all honour" — to Raheel Raza for her unflagging service to interfaith dialogue. May all her ecumenical dreams, and the dreams of those who support her mission, come true in our lifetime.

Barbara Kay

Canadian Opinion Journalist

Introduction

My family and I came to Canada more than 30 years ago from Pakistan because we saw the rise of Islamist fundamentalism in the land of our birth. We never expected that, decades later, we would see the same shoots of Islamism beginning to sprout in the free, liberal-minded and tolerant country we now call our home.

I grew up in a Pakistan that was at the time a pluralistic, visionary country that had tolerance for people of other faiths, which were mostly Christians and Zoroastrians. I am a Muslim, but I studied in a Catholic school. We rarely came across blatant extremism, terrorism, or political Islam.

However, in 1977, Mohammed Zia-ul-Haq took power in a coup. His regime put the elected former prime minister Zulfiqar Bhutto on trial and had him executed. Zia, a follower of Abul Ala Mawdudi, founder of the Islamist party Jamaat-e Islamiyya, implemented his extreme version of Islam. Women had to cover their heads in public, co-education was eliminated in schools, and Friday was made the weekly holiday. Islam, which had never been imposed upon Pakistan's citizens, was suddenly forced into the public sphere. This discomfited those of us who had always lived moderate, normal lives imbued with a traditional, spiritual interpretation of Islam. Zia-ul-Haq was also responsible for implementing, in 1979, the *Hudood Ordinance*. These were Pakistani legal provisions intended to implement Islamic Sharia law. People convicted of robbery were to have their hands or feet cut off. Those found guilty of having pre-marital sex were to be whipped and adulterers would be stoned to death. Blasphemers were threatened with life imprisonment or execution.

The Sharia punishments most heavily targeted women. Women who were victims of rape were imprisoned for adultery. Women were restricted from participating in sports and the media, and head coverings for women were required in public schools and colleges. Women's testimony in court was officially deemed only to be half as credible as men's.

One of the legacies of President Zia was to fan the flames of sectarian differences. I am a Sunni — the majority in Pakistan — married to a Shia man, so we were suddenly living on the edge. In 1979, for the sake of our sanity and well-being, we decided to leave Pakistan. Soon after, attacks against Shias began to rise, culminating in the Gilgit Massacre, where Sunnis, including followers of Osama bin Laden, killed and raped hundreds of Shias, and burned down entire villages.

After a brief stint in Dubai, we applied to immigrate to Canada. The process was smooth because we had the employment prerequisites that Canada needed. The immigration officials who interviewed us painted a glowing picture of Canada and told us about our rights in this country. Not once, however, did officials mention attendant responsibilities.

Initially we were charmed by the concept of official multiculturalism in Canada. As new immigrants, it meant a lot to know that we could preserve our own culture and heritage. We joined the workforce and as we expanded our own horizons, we started seeing signs that something was not right. We found it odd that the Canadian government, in the name of multiculturalism, was giving official government funding to the Pakistani ethnic community to learn their own language and hold "multicultural" events, by their own community, for their own community. Of course, many ethnic groups were taking advantage of this misguided policy, and it was increasingly apparent to us that state-funded multiculturalism was helping to import archaic and centuries-old cultural practices into the Canadian framework without thought of the need to adapt to a new culture. This "excess cultural baggage" was a potentially divisive facet of multiculturalism that, we could tell, promised to split, rather than to build and unite, the people of our new country. We knew too well what had happened in Lebanon, a country that once prided itself on a mosaic of different cultures and faiths co-existing, while happily living in their own enclaves. Eventually a collision between religion and politics exploded into civil war.

One day, the mother of one of my children's classmates of Pakistani origin asked me why my kids sang the Canadian national anthem when it is *haram*, forbidden. Upon asking where she got that information, she confessed that the imam of the local mosque had told the congregation that it was against the faith to sing the national anthem, or indeed to show loyalty to Canada.

Upon investigation, we discovered that some mosques were giving sermons against loyalty to Canada and at other places the sermons were different in English — where they were toned down for outsiders — and Arabic, the more extreme versions meant for the ears of Muslims only. Added to this disagreeable situation was the fact that many immigrants were enforcing cultural values and ideas that were at odds with Canada's established traditions of democracy, freedom, and equality. No government or other authority seemed to contest any of this, and so these messages and teachings began to spread in the communities that had been subject to such instruction.

From a religious perspective, in a strange way it seemed that we were being followed by the same ideology from which we had escaped. One thing we were sure about, having lived and travelled in the Arab world before coming to Canada, was the expanding influence of extremist Muslim politics in Canada, especially among the country's Pakistani Muslims. This was not Islam, but *Islamism*.

Islam is a faith like Judaism and Christianity. Islamism is a political ideology.

Dr. Zuhdi Jasser, a former U.S. Naval officer and a co-founder, along with myself, of the Muslim Reform Movement explains it this way: "Islamist ideas include antipathy for western society, governments, military, and foreign policy. Islamists are misogynists and anti-Semites. They obsess with conspiracy theories and condition Muslims to always be victims and bear grievances against non-Muslims. Islamist grievance groups in the West, such as most Muslim Brotherhood legacy groups, are the first steps in Muslim radicalization."

We began to see the rise of Islamism in Canada manifested in supposedly innocuous cultural nuances — for example, some Pakistani-Canadians dressing like Arabs, resisting western values, expressing hostility toward the principles of freedom and gender equality. We saw many Islamic schools or madrassas being established. When our kids went to university, we learned that the many Muslim Students could be quite outspokenly anti-Semitic and extremist in their views. At York University in Toronto, they often approached my son to convince him to be a better Muslim by joining in congregational prayers instead of going to class. They left nasty notes on my niece's door about how she would burn in hell if she did not wear the hijab. What I saw was a sudden rise of orthodox religiosity amongst young Muslims who were being sucked into the hardline Wahhabi/Salafist ideology.

Stephen Suleyman Schwartz, an American Sufi Muslim journalist and author of *The Two Faces of Islam: The House of Sa'ud from Tradition to Terror*, explains Wahhabism, the religious tendency from which so much of this radicalism seems to spring: "Wahhabism is an extremist, puritanical, and violent movement that emerged, with the pretension of 'reforming' Islam, in the central area of Arabia in the 18th century. It was founded by Ibn Abd al-Wahhab, who formed an alliance with the house of Saud, in which religious authority is maintained by the descendants of al-Wahhab and political power is held by the descendants of al-Saud... From its beginning, Wahhabism declared the entirety of existing Islam to be unbelief, and traditional Muslims to be unbelievers subject to robbery, murder, and sexual violation. Wahhabism has always viewed Shia Muslims genocidally, as non-Muslims worthy of annihilation. Wahhabism has always attacked the traditional, spiritual Islam or Sufism that dominates Islam in the Balkans, Turkey, Central Asia, India, Malaysia, and Indonesia. Wahhabism and neo-Wahhabism (the latter being the doctrines of the Egyptian Muslim Brotherhood and the Pakistani Islamists) are the main source of Islamic extremist violence in the world today. Wahhabism represents a distinct, ultra-radical form of Islamism."

And now it had come to Canada.

I had not set out to be a writer about Islamic issues; my original dream was to be a romantic writer. But when I saw the rise of Wahhabi/Salafism in Canada, I was dismayed. The mainstream non-Muslim community at that time had very little knowledge about Islam. Therefore, I started writing for the *Toronto Star* to educate both Muslims and non-Muslims about the spiritual message of my faith and to encourage my fellow immigrants to embrace the best of Canadian values.

Around the year 2000, I also started writing articles warning Canadian Muslims about the dangers of radicalization, especially among the youth who were confused, with nowhere to go between the mosque and the mall for answers to their questions. They had all the prerequisites to be fodder for Islamist mercenaries looking for victims to brainwash. The youth had grievances, both real and imagined, and the burgeoning number of recruiters offered an ideology they could latch onto. If needed, they would doubtless have Saudi funding to support their nascent extremist viewpoints.

By the late 1990s, several Islamist groups had already infiltrated Canada including Hezbollah and several Sunni Islamic extremist groups, like Hamas, and others with ties to Egypt, Libya, Algeria, Lebanon, and Iran. In 1998, Ward Elcock, then director of the Canadian Security Intelligence Service (CSIS), testified before a Canadian Senate special committee that — with perhaps the exception of the United States — there were more international terrorist organizations active in Canada than in any other country in the world. He said that the counter-terrorism branch of CSIS was investigating over 50 organizations and about 350 individuals.

The earliest Muslims who migrated to Canada came in the late 1800s and early 1900s. They came looking for a better life and many of them settled in the Prairies (the first mosque built in Canada was the Al-Rashid mosque in Edmonton in 1938). They adapted well, some even changing their names to anglicize them. They followed their faith without imposing it on others and were not caught up in dogma and ritual, working side by side with their fellow Canadians.

But by the 1970s, Saudi Arabia was becoming unimaginably rich from its oil exports, and its wealth fueled the spread of Wahhabism to other Muslim lands. So when the second and third waves of Muslim immigrants came to Canada in more recent decades, something had changed. In his 2011 testimony before a Canadian Senate subcommittee, David B. Harris, Canadian lawyer and long-time intelligence specialist, referred to the problem of extremist attitudes being imported by immigrants from certain Muslim-majority countries. Relying on Pew surveys, he observed in the context of the tens of thousands of post-9/11 Egyptian immigrants, that the majority of "Muslim Egyptians prefer Islamists in charge, versus 27% wanting modernizers. Eighty-four percent favour death for converts from Islam, 82% want death for adultery."

In 2009, the extremist Muslim-supremacist group Hizb ut-Tahrir announced it would be holding a public conference in Mississauga, Ontario, where we lived. We immediately tried to convince the mainstream media to report how serious this was (among other things, it plans to take over all countries, including non-Muslim ones by gaining leadership of local communities), but the reporters told us there wasn't much of a story unless there was actually violence afoot, and after all, Hizb-ut Tahrir claims to be "non-violent."

So my husband and I attended the conference undercover. There we heard first-hand how Hizb ut-Tahrir opposition to violence was actually tactical and temporary — that the group is sympathetic to Jihadist ideology and works to create a politically charged atmosphere conducive to terrorism. Hizb ut-Tahrir representatives clearly and confidently stated that it is incumbent on all Muslims to implement Sharia where they live, and to have a Khalifa or Caliph — a sole ruler over all Muslims, guided by Sharia law — from among them.

We were seeing before our own eyes the overt presence of Islamism in Canada that had been gradually infiltrating this country. In December 1999, U.S. Customs officials arrested Ahmed Ressam near Seattle after he came off a ferry from Canada in a car loaded with jars of nitroglycerine, timing devices, and other bomb-making materials, with plans to blow up Los Angeles International Airport.[1] Ressam belonged to a Montreal-based terrorist cell thought to be linked to both the Algerian terrorist group Armed Islamic Group (GIA) and al-Qaeda. In 2006, 17 Muslims, including five juveniles, were arrested in Canada plotting a terrorist attack that involved the storming of Canada's Parliament and the beheading of then prime minister Stephen Harper. Because these were largely "home-grown" Islamic terrorists, some blame was rightly directed towards Canada's decades-old multiculturalism policies. "It's breathtaking that this is going on in Canada," the international trade minister David Emerson told the CBC, "To see the home-grown nature of it is shocking to me." In 2009 Momin Khawaja was the first Canadian to be convicted under Canada's federal anti-terrorism act after being charged with financing and facilitating terrorism.

In August 2010, three Ontario men accused of taking part in a domestic terrorist plot and possessing plans and materials to create makeshift bombs, had allegedly selected specific targets in Canada. In 2013, Chiheb Esseghaier, a Canadian university student, and Raed Jaser, a former Toronto school bus driver, were charged, and eventually sentenced to life in prison for plotting to blow up a passenger train running between Toronto and New York.

The restrictions on Canada's capacity to deal with extremist interlopers are perhaps best illustrated by the family of the late Pakistani immigrant Ahmed Khadr, a senior al-Qaeda operative who used Canada as his base and bolt hole. His son, Omar, was captured after a firefight with American troops in Afghanistan, but now lives in Edmonton. Omar's sister, Zaynab, who had Osama bin Laden at her wedding, publicly expressed her hatred for Canada, while living here, endorsed the 9/11 atrocities and said she hopes her own daughter will die fighting Americans.

---

1   *"Trail of a Terrorist: The Ominous Lesson of Ahmad Rassam."* Cornell University Centre for Middle East Studies *video. October 25, 2001.*

Al-Qaeda is banned in Canada[2] but has Canadian supporters like the Khadr family. Two leaders of Ansar al-Islam are also Canadian and previously lived in Toronto; the group is known for producing chemical and biological weaponry for terrorist purposes. The Armed Islamic Group, which has been in violent conflict with the Algerian government and is banned in Canada, has supporters in Canada's Algerian expatriate community. The Salafist Group for Call and Combat out of North Africa is also banned in Canada, but has members here, nonetheless.

Both Hamas and Islamic Jihad are believed to raise money in Canada, with the Hamas-linked Holy Land Foundation having raised hundreds of thousands of dollars in Canada. Both Hamas and Islamic Jihad terrorist are banned in Canada, but the value in banning terror groups can be limited by the ability of members to change their organizations' names and resume operations. On the website of Public Safety Canada several terrorist groups are listed, some of which are known under different names. Most of them are international Islamic groups. In 2002, the director of CSIS warmed that, "...most of the world's terrorist groups, including al-Qaeda, have adherents in Canada, as they do in every other western democracy. Sunni Islamic terrorist organizations from Algeria, Egypt, Libya and Somalia also have sympathizers in Canada, and we are obliged to deal with that reality."

Indeed, it was already being reported at that time that CSIS's counter-terrorism program was investigating "50 organizational targets and 300 individual targets" in Canada.

The scale of this situation is a reminder of the interplay between radicalism and terrorism, on the one hand, and Canada's enormous per capita immigration on the other. About 260,000 immigrants are admitted each year to Canada, and over 500,000 newcomers per annum, if student and temporary-worker visa-holders are taken into account. Within the immigrant category, tens of thousands seek political asylum and safe haven as refugees. Canada, however, does

---

2   *Don Martin, "Khadrs wave their flag of convenience." National Post, April 15, 2004.*

not automatically detain refuge-seekers upon entry, even those with questionable backgrounds, so thousands of potential terrorists disappear annually into Canada's ethno-cultural communities. For instance, Ahmed Ressam entered Canada in 1994 using a fake French passport and claiming refugee status. Raed Jaser had also used falsified French documents to get into Canada and was able to resist earlier efforts by Canadian authorities to deport him, despite having a criminal record, by claiming, among other things, that he had been harassed by anti-immigrant groups when he lived in Europe.[3]

It is now a crime in Canada to knowingly provide material support to terrorist organizations, including support of a logistical or financial nature. Canada's laws require the publishing of a list of terrorist groups deemed to constitute a threat to the security of Canada and Canadians. Canadian law has also increased the government's investigative powers and paved the way for the country to sign the last two of the United Nations' 12 anti-terrorism conventions.

But vulnerabilities remain. Children can still be brainwashed in certain Canadian Islamic schools, where gender segregation and anti-western lessons are taught. Many Islamic schools around the world, including some in Canada, are foreign-funded, and along with the money comes subversive agendas. And there is little accountability for teachers' credentials in Islamic schools. I was a member of the public committee for the Ontario College of Teachers and was appalled to learn that teachers in the private school system need not be members of the college unless their employers require it. At the Al-Huda Academy, a female-only school in Canada, girls are taught a fundamentalist brand of Islam, promoting polygamy and subservience to men, according to a 2006 report in *Maclean's* magazine.

In some cases, governments in Canada have been co-opted in helping promote radicalization. In 2004, the Ontario government considered implementing "Sharia civil law" in the province after pressure from Islamist groups. Although radical Sharia advocates like the Canadian Council on American-Islamic Relations (CAIR-CAN)

---

3   *Sonja Puzic, "Terror suspect described killing up to 100,000 with bacteria," CTV News, May 9, 2013.*

—now rebranded the National Council of Canadian Muslims — ultimately failed in getting a Sharia victory in the face of public protest, the treatment of the proposition as worthy of discussion has since encouraged Islamists to promote their agendas and become aggressive about bringing in Sharia by stealth. And in 2017, the federal Liberal government passed motion M-103, backed by Liberal MP Iqra Khalid, officially condemning criticism of Islam.

The advent of campus radicalization and foreign funding is a concern that has not been directly, or at least, adequately, addressed by Canadian policymakers and government officials. Some Canadian universities have started establishing chairs in Islamic studies through financing from Arab sources. When the University of Western Ontario's affiliated Huron University College, an Anglican institution, established such a chair in its theology faculty, some alumni protested when it was discovered that a Muslim Brotherhood-oriented organization and the troubling, Virginia-based International Institute of Islamic Thought would provide most of the $2 million in funding for the new chair. Dr. Ingrid Mattson, former head of the Islamic Society of North America, a U.S. organization that was designated by Washington as an unindicted co-conspirator in a history-making terror-funding prosecution, was appointed chair of Huron's Islamic Studies department. Mattson and other radical interests have been able to parlay the ostensible respectability of such appointments into opportunities to gain access to elite circles. Mattson remains chair of the department to this day. And at Carleton University, in Ottawa, the Carleton Centre for the Study of Islam hosted an event for Tariq Ramadan, a personality on the Iranian government's *Press TV,* who is reputed to be a leading Muslim Brotherhood front-person.[4]

The best examples of de-radicalization are those that have involved accountability within pertinent communities. The Tamil and Sikh communities in Canada have managed to some extent to control extremism and terrorism within their ranks. But according to Ahmed Hussen, formerly president of the Canadian Somali Congress and now a federal cabinet minister, the Canadian government was concentrating

---

4   *The Global Muslim Brotherhood Daily Watch, "Tariq Ramadan," nd 2008*

on detecting and arresting terror suspects but leaving their rhetoric unchallenged. Some of the community's youth were being drawn into terrorist activities by Somalia's al-Shabaab terrorist group, the entity reportedly responsible for the 2013 Nairobi shopping-mall massacre.

"The strategy of Canadian officials as they confront this phenomenon in my community has been to view this serious matter only through the prism of law enforcement," said Hussen. "There has not been a parallel attempt to counter the toxic anti-western narrative that creates a culture of victimhood in the minds of members of our community."

But a counter narrative is urgently needed to defeat the voices of those extremists and victim-mongers who prey on Muslim youth, before targeted youth become terrorists. There are few, if any, think tanks in Canada looking in a genuinely realistic way at a long-term vision of the future of Canadian youth, from a counter-radicalization perspective. Contrary to our experience in Canada, the U.K. has had a history of think tanks that have been prepared to deal realistically with threats, and a few of these have pressed government for constructive change. Some British think tanks have produced publications that address some of the key "definers" of terrorism and the rise of radicalization on British university campuses.

Islamism is growing around the world and Canada is no exception. Indeed, Canada is one of its most fertile grounds. Canadians — both Muslim and non-Muslim — must educate themselves about exactly what Islamism is, how it differs from Islam, and the dangerous nature of Islamism. This book comprises a series of articles I have written on that subject in the past, edited, updated and in many places rewritten for this book. I hope it will leave readers with a better understanding of the serious challenge of Islamism, which we all must confront — and fight to stop — together.

"There is a distinction between the faith of Islam and the religionized politics of Islamism, which employs religious symbols for political ends. Many will deny this distinction, including most prominent Islamists themselves. There is no doubt that many Islamists hold the sincere conviction that their Islamism is the true Islam. In fact, however, Islamism emanates from

a political interpretation of Islam: it is based not on the religious faith of Islam but on an ideological use of religion within the political realm. Islamism and Islam are thus different entities, not to be confused with each other..."

Excerpted from Islamism and Islam, *by Bassam Tibi*

A

Anti-Muslim

I am a critic of Islamism. For that, I have been called "anti-Muslim." Those who call me that are usually not even Muslim themselves. How dare they question my faith, my relations with fellow Muslims, my family and my friends? How dare they try to deny me the right to critique those Muslims — those Islamists — who are tarnishing my faith?

What I do is critique. I critique Islamism, passionately, because I believe it is wrong. Because I believe it is bad for Islam. Because I believe it is bad for Muslims. I am pro-Muslim, not anti-Muslim.

I believe in the separation of mosque and state? That does not make me anti-Muslim.

I demand a halt to honour-based violence against women, which includes female genital mutilation, forced and underage marriages and honour killings. This does not make me anti-Muslim.

I believe Sharia governance is incompatible with the Universal Charter of Human Rights and is obsolete. It does not make me anti-Muslim.

I want to defend minorities — like Yazidis — being persecuted by the terrorist group Islamic State and for all minorities living in Muslim lands. And I abhor the human rights violations that many Muslim governments — in Iran, Saudi Arabia, Syria, Turkey, Yemen and others — commit against their own citizens. These things do not make me anti-Muslim.

I work with organizations that are against the spread of a radical Islamist ideology. I call out the danger of radicalization for Muslim youth. I speak out against armed jihad as an obsolete concept from the 7th century used to justify evil terrorism today. I vocally denounce the influence on Muslims of radical Islamists like the Muslim Brotherhood, the Khomeinists and Wahhabists.

In my activist work, I seek to promote peace between faiths. I seek to provide young Muslim men and women a safe space between the mosque and the malls. I encourage reform and reject dogma. I work to make clear the difference between Islam the faith and Islamism the political ideology. I have committed my life to making Muslim communities stronger and better.

If this means I am labelled anti-Muslim then it is a label I am proud of. As the American writer and philosopher Elbert Hubbard said: "Do nothing, say nothing, and be nothing, and you'll never be criticized." I stand for something: I stand against Islamist supremacy and Islamo-fascism and I am doing all I can to fight it.

For the record I've never spoken out against Islam as a faith. Nor for that matter against Judaism, Christianity, Hinduism, Sikhism or any other faith or against those who don't subscribe to any religion.

Here's what it really means to be anti-Muslim:Those who are leading Muslims down a path of perennial victim status, carrying a false flag of Islamophobia, that sets Muslims against the rest of society, that sees the rest of the world as persecutors, that breeds anger, bitterness and weakness. That's what it means to be anti-Muslim.

Anti-Semitism

Anti-Semitism has a direct connection with the rise of Islamism. Islamism is based on an ideology of hate and dehumanization so the Islamists have singled out Jews and Israel as their common enemy. Much of this fanned by the Middle East crisis, while not acknowledging that Middle Eastern Arabs actually make up only a small part of the world's Muslims. Since the creation of Israel, anti-Semitism among Muslims globally has run rampant with Islamists misquoting and misusing time bound Qur'anic passages to further their agenda today.

Islamists often equate anti-Semitism with Islamophobia as a way of promoting their victim ideology. But Islamophobia and anti-Semitism are entirely different. This is why it's important to keep the definition of anti-Semitism in mind.

In June 2019, the government of Canada announced that it was adopting the International Holocaust Remembrance Alliance's (IHRA) definition of anti-Semitism as part of Canada's Anti-Racism Strategy. This is based upon the May 26, 2016 decision in which 31 member states of the International Holocaust Remembrance Alliance (IHRA), of which the United States is a member, adopted a non-legally binding "working definition" of anti-Semitism at its plenary in Bucharest:

"Antisemitism is a certain perception of Jews, which may be expressed as hatred toward Jews. Rhetorical and physical manifestations of antisemitism are directed toward Jewish or non-Jewish individuals and/or their property, toward Jewish community institutions and religious facilities."

The document also says that manifestations might include the targeting of the state of Israel, conceived as a Jewish collectivity. However, criticism of Israel similar to that leveled against any other country cannot be regarded as anti-Semitic.

However, it is anti-Semitic to "(apply) double standards by requiring of (Israel) a behavior not expected or demanded of by any other democratic nation." For example, there are at least 100 land disputes across the globe that are not subject to "BDS" — boycott, divestment and sanctions — movements. Yet, there is unabated rise of the BDS movement targeting Israel across campuses in North America. The BDS movement has been deemed an anti-Semitic movement by the U.S. State Department's definition of anti-Semitism, which has been adopted by 31 other countries and is based on the IHRA's definition of anti-Semitism.

Anti-Semitism frequently charges Jews with conspiring to harm humanity, and it is often used to blame Jews for "why things go wrong." It is expressed in speech, writing, visual forms and action, and employs sinister stereotypes and negative character traits.

As a Muslim living in Canada, I'm really concerned about the rise of anti-Semitism across the globe and especially in North America. I was raised in a Muslim country where no one spoke about Jews or Israel. But I was curious and intrigued after reading The Diary of Anne Frank and Leon Uris's Exodus. So, when we came to Canada, the first chance I got, I went to Israel, and as the cliché goes, the rest is history: I fell in love. Why? Because I found sanity in the madness surrounding this small country and saw true diversity there.

Of course, I can criticize Israeli politics and policy just as much as I criticize the same things here in Canada and in Pakistan, my native land of birth. The freedom of Israelis to criticize their own country is a big part of what makes Israel great. But hatred against a people and a country is never acceptable.

In Canada, according to the organization B'nai Brith, 2,041 incidents of anti-Semitism were recorded in 2019, an increase of 16.5%from the previous year. We see blatant hatred of Jews and Israel being spouted from the mouths of some elected officials. This is a dangerous trajectory. We have learned that hatred leads to dehumanization of "the Other," which leads to violence and eventual genocide. The Holocaust looms as a constant reminder of this.

We need to urgently question why anti-Semitism is rising. And we need to discuss this issue within all communities. This is not just a Jewish problem. It's a humanitarian crisis of huge proportions.

Deborah Lipstadt, a world-renowned Holocaust historian and professor of history at Emory University, said it best in an interview with TVO's Steve Paikin.[5]

"If you're going to fight anti-Semitism, don't fight just because you have a Jewish neighbour or Jewish friends and you don't want them to be hurt or to live in fear. That's good, but that's not the reason. Or, if you're going to fight anti-Semitism just because you hate prejudice against all minorities, religious, ethnic or whatever it might be, that's a good thing, but that's not sufficient... The reason to fight anti-Semitism is that it poses a danger to the democratic societies in which we live. No healthy democratic society can harbour that kind of animus, that kind of hatred and be called a healthy society."

The reasons for the rise in anti-Semitism are many but rarely talked about due to political correctness.

There has been mass immigration to the West from countries that have institutionalized anti-Semitism and teach hatred for Jews even in their school curricula. So those who have grown up on a diet of hate and conspiracy theories bring this ideology with them. We are witnessing this from elected representatives south of the border in America.

With the rise of immigration patterns, the demographics have changed. Western politicians are not only ignoring the rise of anti-Semitism but siding with those who perpetuate it.

Adding insult to injury, the left and Islamists have joined hands to weaponize anti-Semitism. Islamist organizations host the hateful Quds Day rally in major cities — something started by the Iranian regime to protest the existence of Israel and Zionism; ("Quds" is the Arabic name for Jerusalem, which they hope to conquer when their dream of obliterating Israel comes true). Recently, there has been an increase of anti-Semitic attacks by neo-Nazis and white supremacists, who are now using the playbook of the Muslim Brotherhood. This gives the Islamists the excuse of, "It's them — not us," blaming the right wing

---

5   *"The Jews are afraid again,"The Agenda with Steve Paikin, n.d.*

for the rise in anti-Semitism, which is not only inaccurate, but even more dangerous.

The anti-Semitism of neo-Nazi groups are appalling and horrific, but they are localized. A much bigger source of anti-Semitism are the Islamists who are now using the alarm over neo-Nazi groups as a cover to further their own subversive agendas.

B

Blasphemy

In 2014, Meriam Yehya Ibrahim was convicted by courts in Sudan for marrying a Christian man. Ibrahim was raised an Orthodox Christian but, because she was born to a Muslim father, the courts maintained that she was a Muslim, regardless of her personal beliefs. And by marrying a Christian, she was committing "apostasy," the renunciation of Islam. She was also committing "adultery," the courts said, because her marriage to her husband was not legal, and so their relations were forbidden. For the adultery charge she was sentenced to 100 lashes. For apostasy, she was sentenced to death.

Incredibly, Ibrahim and her husband were able to escape Sudan before these brutal sentences could be carried out. And encouragingly, Sudan recently said it will change its blasphemy laws. But the brutal laws there are not an anomoly. In Muslim countries, punishments for blasphemy are used to persecute people — even kill people — who do not adhere to strictly defined definitions of what a Muslim should believe, what they can think, and who they can love.

In my own land of birth, Pakistan an estimated 1,300 people have been charged for blasphemy since 1987. And the numbers are rising every year.

Individual blasphemy cases filed against the minority Ahmadiyya and Christian communities are common knowledge. The case of Asia Bibi, a Christian Pakistani woman, who fled the country after facing a death sentence for blasphemy, made worldwide headlines. But what makes blasphemy laws even more dangerous in the hands of Islamists is that they can be used against anyone the establishment doesn't like. Indeed, the majority of accusations of blasphemy in Pakistan, believe it or not, are against Muslims. And the punishment can range anywhere from a fine to death. Sunni Muslims frequently deploy blasphemy accusations to target Shia Muslims. And all it takes is for some mad mullah to declare a person or community "non-Muslim." Anyone can hurl an accusation of apostasy or blasphemy on his or her neighbour, friend or fellow citizen with impunity. This is just one of the many ways that Islamism hurts Muslims, as well as other religions.

In one case, Pakistani police arrested 68 lawyers who were protesting the arrest of a colleague. Because the lawyers as part of the protest were chanting their colleague's name, "Umar," which happens to also to be the name of a revered figure in the Qur'an (Umar was a companion of the Prophet Muhammed), police deliberately misconstrued their words, and charged them with blasphemy. In another case, a mother who called her son, who was named Muhammed, a "devil" for misbehaving was charged with blasphemy against the Prophet. That's all it takes. Almost anyone on the street can be charged at any time, any place.

The same is true in Afghanistan, Iran, Saudi Arabia and Nigeria, where blasphemy is punishable by execution. But many more Muslim countries criminalize blasphemy and punish it severely.

Probably in all those countries, and certainly where I come from, if you asked the average person if they know why blasphemy laws exist, they would no doubt say they believe it is part of the Qur'an. In their minds, they are following Islam in implementing and supporting these horrific laws.

However, that is simply not true. The concepts of blasphemy and apostasy are definitely not supported by the Qur'an, which clearly indicates "there is no compulsion in religion." Blasphemy laws came into being after Muhammed died, when some who had sworn allegiance to him and converted to Islam for him had, after his death, tried to renounce being Muslim. The leaders who followed Muhammed saw that as a direct threat to their power and so made up a law that blasphemy — by converting, among other things — would be punishable by death.

The blasphemy law is contrary to every aspect of universal human rights. Blasphemy laws are in violation of articles 2, 3 and 4 of the UN Declaration on the Elimination of All Forms of Intolerance and Discrimination based on Religion and Belief and also violates articles 2 and 4 of the Declaration of the Rights of Persons Belonging to National, Ethnic, Religious and Linguistic Minorities.

It's been 1,400 years since Muhammad died. But blasphemy laws are still here, and if some Islamists have their way, these appalling laws will only become more common. In 2009, Pakistan presented a resolution to the UN Human Rights Commission in Geneva calling upon the world to formulate laws against the defamation of religion. Rather than rethinking their backwards, brutal blasphemy laws, these Islamists want to spread them around the world. It is up to world powers and countries that give huge amounts of aid to these countries with inhumane blasphemy laws to do something to stop them.

Burqas

We should ban the burqa.

Most Canadians who might agree with that would probably be afraid to say it, because they know they'll be accused of being Islamophobic. But I'm a Muslim. And I think we shouldn't be afraid to say it. We should ban the burqa, the all-encompassing cloth garment

31

that covers every inch of a woman, including just a screen for her eyes. And we should ban the niqab, which covers everything on a woman except the eyes.

These body coverings have nothing at all to do with Islam. They're a symbol of Islamism — the hatred of and control over women. So I am astonished to see our politicians and our courts caving in to Islamists who have nothing but contempt for Canada's values of gender equality.

I never saw these garments when I was growing up in Karachi, Pakistan. But in the 30 years I have called Canada home, I have seen a steady rise of Muslim women being strangled in the pernicious black tent that is passed off to naïve and guilt-ridden white, mainstream Canadians as an essential Islamic practice.

They are no such things. These smothering fabrics are the political flags of radical Islamist groups like the Muslim Brotherhood, ISIS, the Taliban, al-Qaida and the Wahhabists of Saudi Arabia. So not only do anti-Islamist Muslims like me now have to fight against the medieval theocrats who claim to represent my faith, to find a safe space in Islam. We now also have to battle the Canadian courts, who have come to the defense of these misogynist face masks.

Consider the case of Zunera Ishaq, a woman who emigrated to Canada from Pakistan in 2008. After previously showing her face to a Canadian immigration official in 2013 when taking her Canadian citizenship test, she later refused to take part in the citizenship ceremony because she would have to show her face while taking the oath. The federal government, under former prime minister Stephen Harper, had rightly made it illegal to wear face coverings during citizenship ceremonies. But in 2015, the Federal Court overruled that.

Unbelievably, this makes Canada even more regressive than fundamentalist Islamic countries. Even in the jihadi badlands of Peshawar, the chief justice of the high court ordered female lawyers not to wear face veils in courtrooms. The judge had good reason for his decision, saying that veils made it impossible to identify who was whom.

He clearly knew something that Canadian judges don't: that covering the face is not a religious requirement for Muslim women. It's true the Qur'an calls for modest dress, for men and women. But that has nothing to do with covering one's face. Some Muslim women interpret this as covering their hair, with a scarf or chador. But as the scholar of Islamic history, Prof. Mohammad Qadeer of Queen's University wrote in *The Globe and Mail* in March 2006: "The argument about concealing one's face as a religious obligation, is contentious and is not backed by the evidence."

He added, "in Western societies, the niqab also is a symbol of distrust for fellow citizens and a statement of self-segregation. The wearer of a face veil is conveying: 'I am violated if you look at me.'... It is a barrier in civic discourse. It also subverts public trust."

And that is why veils should be banned. But two of Canada's political parties have been fighting against any such ban. The federal Liberals and NDP are treating Canada's burqists as a latter-day Rosa Parks, fighting for justice. They are no such thing. Those who want to see niqabs and burqas on Canadian streets are fighting for Islamism.

There is just one way forward: The next government must legislate the complete ban on wearing face masks in public. To expose the hypocrisy of the Islamists — and for the sake of Canada's security.

C

Caliphate

"As Western Governments including the Australian Government work hard to frustrate the uprising and maintain their stranglehold over the Muslim world, we must work even harder for the liberation and return to Islam."

If you think the above words read like the raving of a Taliban fanatic in a cave somewhere in Afghanistan, think again. Those words are from the official launch material of the Khilafah Conference 2011 — "Uprisings in the Muslim Word... on the road to Khilafah." A "khalifah" is another word for a caliphate — the one-man rule of a Muslim leader. And the conference was held in Sydney, Australia by the local chapter of Hizb ut-Tahrir, a global fundamentalist, anti-Christian, anti-Semitic Islamist group that aims at nothing less than creating a caliphate that controls the entire world and is so extreme that it's been banned in Germany, Russia, China, Egypt, Turkey, Pakistan and even most Arab countries.[6]

---

6   David Commins, "Taqi Al-Din Al-Nabhani and the Islamic Liberation Party," The Muslim World 81, no.3-4 (1991): 194-211.

Sitting thousands of miles away in Canada I, as a Canadian Muslim on the front lines of the battle against radical jihad in the West, was not only appalled when I saw this, but shocked. Hizb ut-Tahrir— one of the most reviled and feared Islamist groups in central Asia — was allowed to hold a huge conference in Australia where the entire mandate is anti-western propaganda and dialogue about establishing a Muslim caliphate.

Hizb ut-Tahrir has also met in Canada, in the Toronto area, in 2009. I attended the conference undercover, as you can read about in the introduction to this book. And the message I heard was clear: That it's incumbent on every Muslim living in a non-Muslim land to impose Sharia law and to work towards an Islamic state. This, by the way, is actually contrary to the teaching of the Qur'an, which advises Muslims to follow the laws of the lands in which they live.

In Canada we've fought hard for equality, democracy and freedoms — all of which are anathema to Islamists. The same is true in Australia and every western country that these extremists want to see turned into caliphates. Yet Islamists have no qualms about using the same freedoms they decry to promote their message — a message to end our freedoms and impose Sharia rule and tyranny.

Christchurch

The Christchurch massacre at two New Zealand mosques in March 2019 was a horrific, xenophobic attack against Muslims. Fifty-one people were murdered, 49 more were injured. The killer publicized that he wanted to kill Muslims.

From every tragedy there are lessons to be learned, even this one. And in many Muslim communities, after the initial shock and sympathy, the Christchurch attack was turned by Islamists into an obscene political move.

The rhetoric became one of a singular victim ideology. The common thread running through the Islamist narrative is that anyone or any organization that ever critiqued radical Islam or Islamism is somehow to blame for the Christchurch mosque attack. This includes reformist Muslims who, for a very long time, have been challenging radical Islam and its takeover of the Muslim narrative. Chelsea Clinton was accosted by campus radicals at a candlelight vigil for the Christchurch victims. They blamed her for the attack because she had recently denounced anti-Semitism when Ilhan Omar, the U.S. member of Congress, had made the bigoted statement that American politicians only supported Israel because they were controlled by Jewish money. "This right here is the result of a massacre stoked by people like you and the words that you put out into the world," one student lectured Clinton, who was three months pregnant at the time. "I want you to know that and I want you to feel that deep inside. The 49 people died because of the rhetoric you put out there."

In an op-ed in *The New York Times*, Toronto writer Omer Aziz[7] accused certain intellectuals, including Canada's Jordan Peterson and the American neuroscientist Sam Harris, of playing a role in the massacre, because they had criticized the overuse of "Islamophobia" as an accusation against anyone who dared to criticize anything about Islam. Without realizing the irony, Aziz's comrades on the left began circulating lists of names of other people who needed to be purged from society because they had said things insufficiently respectful of Islamophobia or Islam. Or perhaps, like Clinton, had simply offended Islamists by denouncing anti-Semitism.

Tellingly, ISIS spokesman Abu Hassan al-Muhajir spoke out, after months of silence, to call for something similar. "The scenes of the massacres in the two mosques should wake up those who were fooled and should incite the supporters of the caliphate to avenge their religion." He no doubt envisioned a more literal purge of the politically incorrect infidels than his left-wing allies had in mind when they made their hitlist, but it's clear both were on the same team.

---

7   *Omar Aziz, "Our brother, our executioner," New York Times, March 16 2019.*

But the cries of "Islamophobia" by the Islamists completely obscured the fact that Muslims who live in western societies enjoy full rights and freedoms — rights and freedoms that are, almost without exception, better than what they would enjoy in Muslim-controlled countries. Aside from a few xenophobic attacks, which should always be condemned, Muslims are part of the larger landscape and have been successful in getting their reasonable — and unreasonable — accommodation needs fulfilled as citizens of a western democracies with full rights.

What seems to have been missed in the larger conversation is the idea of how a humanitarian and visionary western leader like New Zealand's prime minister, Jacinda Ardern, deals with a minority population in her country. Muslims comprise approximately one per cent of New Zealand's population. Yet the outreach, sympathy and empathy that other New Zealanders have shown them in their time of mourning has been unprecedented. In fact, Ardern showed so much sympathy — she even put on a hijab — that some Muslims felt she should convert to Islam. They even asked her to do so (which points to the narrow and one-sided vision of the world they hold).

Ardern's behavior points to a larger conversation we should be having — but aren't —about how Muslim-majority societies deal with their own minorities, particularly in contrast to how western countries accept Muslims. The track record is pathetic:

- In Pakistan, Christians and the minority Ahmaddiya community are continuously persecuted for their faith. Hindu girls and women are frequently[8] kidnapped and forcibly converted to Islam.

- In a predominately Muslim town in southern Ethiopia, a Muslim crowd burned 10 churches of eight different Christian denominations.

---

8 *"Hindu girls continue to be abducted, converted to Islam in the complicit state of Pakistan," Sirf News Network, May 4, 2020.*

38

- In Sudan, Christians and minority Muslim tribes are being persecuted and killed.

- In Egypt, numerous Coptic Christian churches have been destroyed. Copts live in constant fear of their women being kidnapped and forcibly converted.

- The most victimized and persecuted people in the world today are Christians living in the Middle East.

The point being is that if we are ever to learn from a tragedy, Christchurch should speak to the difference between how minorities are treated in western countries such as New Zealand when they are in need, compared to how minorities are treated in Muslim-majority countries.

If Muslim leaders admire Jacinda Arden so much, then they should copy her example and give their minorities the dignity and respect they deserve.

Clergy

In 2019, Tehran confirmed that it had exceeded the 300 kilograms of low-enriched uranium it had been allowed to produce under the 2015 nuclear deal it had made with the Obama administration and the EU — and, by doing so, acknowledged that the Iranian regime had been lying all along about its nuclear intentions.

This is not the first time the ayatollahs have deceived the world about their plans. They lie habitually about this, although they consider themselves divinely appointed as God's vice-regents on earth.

They call themselves Supreme Council leaders and Grand Ayatollahs. They are neither "supreme" nor "grand," because they will lie through the teeth for their own subversive agendas — mainly, to bring down Israel and the West.

This brings me to the question of the role of Muslim clergy in the area of Islamic reform.

For a long time, we reformist Muslims believed that change will only come when the Islamic leaders — that is, imams — joined the reform movement and start making statements about the urgent need for change from within the faith.

However, we eventually realized that this was not going to happen. Genuine and committed reformers have not been the clergy people, but members of civil society who have put their lives on the line to speak about change.

The Christian Reformation is an example of civil society championing a reform movement and passionately pursing it. Some of the Hindu reforms, like abolishing the practice of sati or suttee (the burning of widows), also came from civil society reformers like Ram Mohan Roy.

The reason most imams are not on board the reform movement is simple: For them, it's all about the money.

There are two kinds of imams: For Shiites, they are ayatollahs who receive khums, a tax paid by all Shiites. For Sunnis, there are Saudi (Wahhabist) imams who collect zakat and fitra (forms of compulsory charity). In both cases, the imams are collectively raking in trillions of dollars from Muslims around the world.

Then there are imams who travel the globe in their turbans and frocks pretending to be moderate. They will say exactly what you want to hear, but are always loyal to their base. However, when they shake your hand, the other hand is in your wallet or purse. Even while speaking in western countries to diverse audiences, they don their cloak and turban as a way of dressing up their legitimacy.

When my family first came to Canada, we attended an Islamic Centre in Ontario. At that time, it was a moderate place of worship with an imam who was a professor at a university. The sermon was in English and was inclusive. But since then, Iran has been using its money to control the messages coming out of Shiite mosques. The imam there has since praised Iran's supreme leader Ayatollah Khameini in his sermons.

"These are the type of leaders that Allah wants to see," the Imam said, according to a report in Jihad Watch. "It is our responsibility to support them and to pray for them." This is the same Ayatollah Khameini who has branded Israel as "barbaric," "infanticidal" and the "sinister, unclean rabid dog of the region."

Years ago, I met another alleged reformer who ended up turning Islamist: UCLA law professor Khaled Abou El Fadl, whom I once interviewed. At the time, I thought he was a visionary in his teachings about how to reform Islam. Since then, he has expressed support for the Muslim Brotherhood in Egypt. In 2019, the Middle East Forum reported that he was banned by the Islamic Center of Southern California from hosting a sermon praising the Muslim Brotherhood leader Mohamed Morsi, Egypt's short-lived president, after Morsi's death.[9]

In response, an indignant Abou El Fadl posted a rambling 50-minute video on YouTube, in which he praised Morsi as a "martyr," while calling the Islamic Centre of Southern California's leaders "authoritarian and despotic garbage," "ignorant idiots" and "an embarrassment to Islam."

As with many, it seems, he is moderate no more.

To be fair, there are actually a few imams truly interested in reform. You can spot them by the way they don't dress: they shed their garb of Islamist religiosity because they know it is the garb of theocracy, misogyny and abuse of human rights.

---

9   *Sam Westrop, "Islamist Identity Troubles," The Rabwah Times, July 3, 2019.*

D

Deflection

I once sat on a radio panel about Islamic Sharia law, featuring two academics from American universities: a Muslim professor of Islamic studies and a Christian professor of religious studies. Both spent the entire program trying to deflect from the real issues we must face when it comes to Sharia. For many Muslims, and especially Muslim organizations, a discussion about Islam and Muslims usually ends up in defence and deflection. Deflection is what apologists for extremist forms of Islam do best. And that is the biggest obstacle standing in the way of achieving true Islamic reform, and the rejection of Islamism.

Rather than talking about the violations of human rights happening under Sharia, the professors spent their time preoccupied with discussing "The Golden Age of Islam" and "How Christianity went through a similar crisis" and other similarly irrelevant information. The question of real focus should have been: "What is happening in the name of Islam today and what do we do about the atrocities being perpetrated in the name of Sharia as we speak?"

43

It is our moral and ethical responsibility, as Muslims, to discuss and debate these issues — even though they may be considered our "dirty laundry."

But how are we going to get there when the only picture most Muslims want to paint is one of grandeur and glory of the past? One way is to take a step-by-step factual look at what is actually taking place in Muslim lands.

Such as: In April 2014, 276 schoolgirls were kidnapped in the north of Nigeria by a radical Islamist group, Boko Haram, whose name, loosely translated, means "western education is forbidden." The terrorists said they would sell the girls as slaves, force them into marriage and convert those who are Christian to Islam. Some of the girls have since been found, some have been released, and some were rescued, but more than 100 are still missing.

Or: On September 21, 2013, four terrorist gunmen said to be representing al-Shabab, a jihadist fundamentalist group allied with al-Qaida, attacked the upscale Westgate Mall in Nairobi, Kenya. The attack killed 62 civilians and five Kenyan soldiers and wounded 200 others. The president of Kenya, Uhunu Kenyatta, promised, "We shall hunt down the perpetrators wherever they run to. We shall get to them and we shall punish them for this heinous crime. ...They want to cause fear and despondency in our country, but we will not be cowed." About al-Shabab, he added, "Terrorism is a philosophy of cowards."

Kenyetta addressed the problem head-on. But then, Kenyatta is not a Muslim, or the leader of a Muslim country (only about 11%of Kenyans are Muslim; most, like Kenyatta, are Christian). Leaders of Muslim countries and the OIC have let us down when it comes to fighting extremism. They frequently object to use of the word "terrorist" when it is attached to Muslims. They deflect. How much more bloodshed and carnage do we have to endure before we wake up to the reality that something dangerous has taken root in the heart of the Muslims who kill in the name of faith?

There are some pressing questions we Muslims must ask. Our faith as practiced today doesn't readily embrace humanity, modernity, music, arts or literature, but it counts among its adherents the Islamists who defend or even embrace violence, terror and murder.

Why is it, for example, that when there is even a single death in the "conflict in the Middle East," Muslims in Pakistan will beat their chests, run out on the street, and rally with slogans calling for the death of the U.S. and Israel — but they stay home and stay quiet when their own countrymen massacre entire families of Christians and destroy churches?

And why it that Middle Eastern Muslims do not even bat an eyelash over death squads against Shia Muslims and the persecution of Ahmadiyya Muslims? Where is the denunciation by our clergymen from the pulpit?

Why is that so many mullahs, particularly online, enjoy support for their warped interpretation of the Qur'an, insisting that armed jihad is valid and necessary?

Platitudes about Islam being a faith of peace are not credible anymore. Deflection is the shield of Islamism. The name of Islam is only as good as the way its followers practice it. If we allow Muslims continue to kill in the name of Islam, then Islam will be recognized by the deflection and silence of those who did not speak out when their faith is being massacred as Islamists massacre humanity.

E

Extremism

In September 2012, I addressed the UN Human Rights Council in a joint statement with the International Humanist and Ethical Union, on the subject of extremism in Islam. The International Humanist and Ethical Union is a global umbrella human-rights organization with a membership of over 160 groups in 80 countries. The subject at that time was reports on Islamic extremism in Somalia and Northern Mali, but as I told the Human Rights Council, Islamic extremism is a serious and dangerous problem worldwide. And a big part of the reason for that is the role played by none other than the Organization for Islamic Cooperation (OIC), the so-called "collective voice" of the Islamic world. It is, in fact, the voice of the extremists in Islam, controlled and funded as the OIC is by the Wahhabist-influenced Sharia regime in Saudi Arabia.

Below is a transcript of my remarks from nearly a decade ago. Unfortunately, the substance of our statement is just as relevant today:

Madam President

The reports on Somalia [A/HRC/21/36] and Northern Mali [A/HRC/21/64] highlight a far wider problem that we are also witnessing in Libya, Iraq, Iran, Egypt, Pakistan and Saudi Arabia: the excesses of those dedicated to violent, extremist interpretations of Islam. The destruction of Sufi shrines and the imposition of strict Sharia in northern Mali; the targeted killings already this year of more than 400 Shia Muslims in Pakistan, and the appalling use of blasphemy laws in Saudi Arabia and Pakistan to silence, imprison and incite violence against those of different faiths, are all symptoms of this disease. When and how did the religion of peace become transformed into a religion of violence and extremism? Well, Madam President, we don't have very far to look.

For more than 30 years, extremist interpretations of Islam have been promoted and funded by Saudi Arabia, a member State of this Council. Can the failure of the OIC to effectively tackle this problem possibly be related to the fact that the OIC itself receives substantial funding from the same source? Madam President, extremism and violence carried out in the name of Islam are doing more than any actions of the West to fan the flames of hatred against Islam. Since 1979 the benign faith of our grandparents has been hijacked by politicians, governments and well-funded militias to promote extremism, violence and terror.So the key question for the OIC is this: Will they continue to bleat about Islamophobia in the West whilst ignoring Islamic extremism at home, or is it too much to hope that they will finally decide that enough is enough, and take positive steps to tackle the problem at its source?

Thank you, Madam President.

F

Fatwa

A fatwa on moi? It's true. I once received a fatwa against an annual event I host. A fatwa is "a non-binding legal opinion issued in response to a legal problem."

But fatwas can be much more political — and sometimes much more dangerous — than that definition makes them sound. Iraqi Islamist jurists issued a fatwa in the 1930s that called on Muslims to boycott Zionist products. In 2004, an Egyptian Islamic scholar issued a fatwa to boycott all American and Israeli products. Osama bin Laden issued what he called a fatwa (although he wasn't a legal scholar) declaring a "jihad against Jews and Crusaders."

And most famously, there was the one issued by Iran's Ayatollah Khomeini, who, in his role as a mufti, frequently issued fatwas. In 1989, he issued a fatwa calling for the death of Indian-born novelist Salman Rushdie, for blasphemy, over his book *The Satanic Verses*, which was inspired by the life of the Prophet Muhammed. Khomeini then issued a second fatwa offering a multimillion-dollar reward for killing "any of those involved in its publication who are aware of its content." Rushdie dodged several assassination attempts. His Japanese translator, just 44 years old, was stabbed to death.

(Note that in his book "Fatwa: Violence and Discourtesy" reviewed by Dr. Daniel Pipes in Middle East Quarterly, author Mehdi Mozaffari argues that Khomeini did not see this pronouncement as a *fatwa* (he made only one glancing reference to it as such) and in fact, the edict in many ways does not fit the mold of a *fatwa*: it was not in response to a question, it was not handwritten, it was neither signed nor sealed, and as his country's ruler, Khomeini was specifically disbarred from issuing a *fatwa*. Mozaffari refers to it as a 'payam' (message).

The fatwa against me was certainly less lethal. It was an order against celebrating Milaad, an event that features poetry or literature written in honour of the Prophet Muhammad's birth, his life and achievements. Milaad is a spiritual tradition developed by Muslims out of love and reverence for the Prophet and his family, although it is not a religious duty. I've celebrated Milaad since I was a child. Back then, there were no extremists hounding us trying to ban it.

I knew that sooner or later some religious crank would find me. But still, I was surprised when I saw the e-mailed fatwa with my name on it.

I'm no stranger to hostility: I've been pepper sprayed; received crank calls and hate mail; my husband has been taken aside and asked why he "allows" his wife so much freedom to speak out. At various times people have suggested that I write under a pseudonym or change my name entirely. But I give Canada credit for giving me courage to live freely, speak my mind and celebrate the way I choose. Only when I came here did I find freedom and confidence as a Muslim woman to study and understand that my faith, Islam, does not bind me but frees me to pursue knowledge and strengthen my spirituality regardless of my gender.

The resulting liberation of my mind has also allowed me to reflect upon and critique some of the false ideologies being promoted by my co-religionists, especially those who take direction from the political Islamism that forms the state religion of Saudi Arabia and makes a mockery of our faith. I've spoken out about injustices against women and minorities, about gender equality, against intolerance, against extremism and violence, and, most often, about inflexible interpretations of Islam that force all joy out of our traditions.

A year prior to getting my fatwa, I had read a report in an ethnic newspaper about a strict message from Sheik Abdel Azeez al-Sheikh, the grand mufti and highest religious official in Saudi Arabia. He blasted Milaad celebrations as heresy and said those who observe these traditions are "mimicking Christians."

So, I promptly wrote an article for the *Toronto Star* and explained the history of the Milaad tradition, placing it at the time of the Prophet and explaining that it's a custom that was developed out of love for our Prophet.

But the next time I sent out invitations to my annual Milaad celebration, one of them made its way to the U.S.-based Al-Amana, or American Muslim Association of North America. Al-Amana, it turns out, offers an online fatwa service: "Fatwas by Al-Amana Shura advisers," they advertise. "We search before giving a fatwa." They also have a toll-free hotline: 1-800-95-FATWA. No joke.

According to their rather lengthy, incredibly boring fatwa e-mail, I've received ruling #2/882. And I ignored it. I went ahead and had my celebration. What better way to say a thank-you to God than celebrating over samosas and tea, with my friends, family and well-wishers?

Islamists might take these kinds of fatwas seriously. Muslims shouldn't. There are plenty of better things to issue fatwas against, like subjugating women, for instance. Or extrajudicial killings of journalists and dissidents in Muslim countries. Or the persecution of non-Muslims. When groups like Al-Amana and the other muftis get around to those, then maybe then their fatwas will be worth listening to.

Female Genital Mutilation

The World Health Organization (WHO) reports that more than 125 million girls and women across the globe have been horrendously abused in a practice known as female genital mutilation (FGM). FGM is comprised of all procedures that involve partial (or total) removal of the external female genitalia. The term also covers other injury to the female genital organs for non-medical reasons.

While FGM is not mentioned in the Qur'an, it is practiced by many Muslim communities (and non-Muslims as well). The Islamists subscribe to some Hadiths (or, secondary texts) that are not credible or validated. Muslim scholars, while not condoning it, by and large do not openly condemn the practice either. This gives the Islamist clerics the cover to accept this barbaric practice continuing under their noses ostensibly for "health" and "religious" reasons. But it is well-known that the real purpose behind it is to curtail women's sexuality.

This brutal and cruel practice is most popular in Muslim countries, but Muslims are spreading it to even those countries where women are supposed to have full human rights. The award-winning 2013 documentary *Honor Diaries* helped expose the ongoing illegal practice of FGM in many western countries, including the U.S. Until then, there had been very little public awareness of it in the West. It is shockingly estimated that around 200,000 girls in the U.S. are at risk of being forced to undergo this procedure. This can either happen on U.S. soil or they are sometimes sent on "cutting vacations" to the Middle East or Africa. —- taking children back to their native countries during the summer break to undergo this barbaric procedure.

FGM is a horrendous, harmful and painful cultural practice. It can cause girls and women to bleed dangerously, become infertile, suffer permanent physical and psychological damage and sometimes even die from the side effects. Most victims will remain under the radar until a medical doctor sees them. In most cases, they don't see a doctor at all, and the practice remains largely unreported.

It was not until 2008 that the WHO, together with nine other United Nations partners, issued a statement about eliminating FGM. In 2010, the WHO, in collaboration with other key UN agencies and international organizations, published a "Global strategy to stop health care providers from performing female genital mutilation." In 2012, the UN General Assembly adopted a resolution on the elimination of FGM.

Although FGM is illegal in Canada, the practice continues among immigrant communities. In 2011, nearly 29,000 women from Africa and the Middle East became permanent residents of Canada. A female doctor who has worked with hundreds of immigrant women says a high percentage of these girls and women would have undergone FGM by the end of that summer. Thousands more were at risk.

In the United States, the problem of FGM is no better. According to the latest statistics from the Population Reference Bureau, more than half a million girls and women are at risk of FGM. Today there is more public awareness about this horrific practice, thanks to the ceaseless work of activists such as Jaha Dukureh, an Atlanta-based FGM survivor. She found the courage to stand up and the strength to speak out after seeing the *Honor Diaries* documentary. She then successfully petitioned the White House to investigate the prevalence of FGM in America.

One country that has made progress in stopping this terrible practice is Burkina Faso, where three out of four girls and women have undergone FGM. Chantal Compaoré, the wife of former president Blaise Compaoré, began an African-led movement for change, resulting in a UN General Assembly resolution, led by the Africa Group, calling for a global ban on the practice in December 2012. Chantal Compaoré played a vital role in driving this resolution and has been dedicated to ending FGM in her country for more than 20 years, resolving to help eradicate FGM within one generation.

In the United States and Canada, we need more awareness and education about the practice of FGM to ensure that everyone, from policymakers to educators, is aware of the practice. We need to shine a light on this practice, with public discussion about ways to stop this cruel and inhuman phenomenon.

G

Gender Jihad

Here's an interesting anecdote. A few years before the U.S. invasion of Afghanistan, Barbara Walters went to the Taliban-controlled country for a story on gender roles. She noted that women customarily walked five paces behind their husbands. After the overthrow of the oppressive Taliban regime, Walters went back to Afghanistan for a follow-up story, and was surprised to notice that many women were happy to maintain the old custom of walking behind their husbands, sometimes even further back than before. She approached one of the Afghani women and asked, "Why do you now seem happy with the old custom that you once tried so desperately to change?" The woman looked Walters straight in the eyes, and without hesitation, said, "Land mines!"

That's a joke that was making the rounds some years ago. In reality, the stereotypical images westerners might have of Muslim women shadowing their husbands in black shrouds, walking behind them or seated behind them in the back seats of cars, are not even remotely reflective of the lives of Muslim women in general.

And headlines in the mainstream media that have reduced Muslim female identity to their submission to men, as symbolized most visibly by their clothing — the veil — aren't any more helpful. It's rare to hear any discussion about Muslim women that doesn't include that four-letter word. TV, films and books like "Beyond the Veil" and "Behind the Veil" have started to border on the ridiculous. Coming soon: "Rebel without a Veil" and "Whose Veil is it Anyway?"

What's important to note about the fight against Islamism is that, when it comes to women's rights, the revolution isn't about reinventing these rights. It's about reclaiming them. Muslims come from almost 60 countries of the world, so they reflect a rich and diverse cultural mosaic. Like the differences in our language, food and clothing from one region to another, Muslim women are also diverse, coming from African, Arab, Asian, European or North American backgrounds. So it wasn't Islam that turned women into those submissive stacks of laundry with legs we too frequently see represented in the media. Islamism did that.

The Arab world before the advent of Islam was a crude tribal society where women were sold as slaves, where men kept hundreds of wives and concubines, where women were considered to lack a human soul, and where newly born girls brought shame and were frequently buried alive. It was in this atmosphere that the message of Islam was sent as a blessing for women, finally giving them rights to inheritance, divorce and marriage, keeping their own name and their earned wages, meagre as they might have been. They could participate in battle. They could have an abortion up to the fourth month of pregnancy and birth control was permitted. This was in the 7th century. It would be over a thousand years later before Canadian women were legally declared "persons," and women in Britain were given the right to keep their earned wages.

Let me tell you about some early Muslim women who are role models for us. The Prophet's first wife, Khadijah, was a successful businesswoman who was approximately 12 years older than the Prophet and sent a proposal of marriage to him. His second wife, Lady Ayesha, led a war and rode into combat on a camel. It has been said that when the Prophet's daughter Fatema entered the room, the Prophet stood up in respect. Fatema was a mesmerizing public speaker and her sermons have been recorded in historical documents. Rabia of Basra, a female Muslim saint, was the first mystic of Islam.

You can see where I'm going with this. I want you to understand the power that Muslim women once had.

A considerable number of women of the 9th and 10th Centuries are mentioned in the Arabic and Persian sources for their extraordinary achievements in mysticism, as well as being poets, calligraphers or jurists. Bilqees, the Queen of Sheba, exemplifies the role of important women in the history of Muslims. She was a ruler who consulted with her people before making important decisions. She travelled to Jerusalem to visit King Solomon, drawn by his fame, and bearing a caravan of valuables and spices, to test him with difficult questions. She made decisions for herself and her people, not hiding behind walls, or standing behind a man.

As we look into the hidden pages of history, we find many powerful Muslim women who were leaders. In political life, there have been no less than 40 female Muslim heads of state. Fifteen of them were formal sultanas or queens who had the khutba (Friday sermon) pronounced in their names and whose insignia was minted on coins.

That was then. Now we encounter hardly a single Islamic woman jurist. Women are all but absent from Islamic public and intellectual life. There are several reasons for this alarming phenomenon. A particularly disturbing one is the derogatory cultural attitude that seems to have infected many Muslim men. Very few are willing to be instructed or taught by women. Muslim men, in North America and elsewhere, seem to have developed a misogyny that consistently aspires to exclude women from conferences, meetings, gatherings, and even the mosques.

The fact is that, despite what the Islamists claim, Islam neither limits women to the private sphere, nor does it give men supremacy over public and private life.

But the rights, responsibilities and roles of Muslim women are now decided by men or interpreted through a male lens. Essentially, Muslim women have remained pawns to cultural interpretations, despite the fact that Islam as a faith and a divine message gave them many rights. Most accepted translations have been done by men because women were excluded from the foundational discourse. Their voicelessness during critical periods of development of the Qur'anic interpretation and lawmaking has created a crisis of religious identity where they are still being told about their rights — or lack of them.

Today when a Muslim woman speaks out or is qualified to take a leadership role, she is called a militant feminist. If she speaks in ways expected of women, she is seen as an inadequate leader. If she speaks in ways expected of leaders, she is seen as an inadequate woman.

Ironically, it was western colonization that worsened the discrimination and victimization of women. Europeans brought their own sexist attitudes and practices to Muslim lands (for example, their rules about how men must control all the financial affairs of the household). Muslim men used their new power to keep depriving women of their rights, using male-centric religious interpretations to legitimize their actions.

Constant exploitation of women in Islamic societies is not religious, but cultural. It stems from the huge chasm between the faith and our knowledge of the faith — between theory and practice.

Michael Ross, a UCLA political science professor, noted in a 2008 paper[10] that women have made less progress towards gender equality in the Middle East than anywhere else in the world. He quotes UN statistics that show the level of education among Arab women is the lowest in the Muslim world. But it isn't Islam that causes this, he argues. It has more to do with strong patriarchal norms, laws and political institutions. And since the rise of petro-Islam, the easy oil wealth that flowed into Arab Gulf countries made it easier for them to sideline women from the economy, reducing female power and solidifying male power.

---

10   *Michael Ross, "Oil, Islam, and women," American Political Science Review, 102, no. 1 (2008): 107-123.*

The good news is that today, many female Muslim scholars have initiated groundbreaking steps towards setting the record straight. Their work is referred to as "gender jihad" (one meaning of "jihad" being "a struggle to overcome injustice"). And their fight is literally one of life and death. Muslim women in oppressive countries often live on the edge of despair, living their lives amid wars, lack of food, lack of clean water, or lack of shelter. Gender justice is an issue Muslims must face if they ever hope to thrive.

Naturally the self-appointed caretakers of Muslim traditionalism feel threatened by the phenomenon that a significant number of women are now seen in spaces normally thought of as for men only. They see emancipated Muslim women as a decadent and dangerous symbol of corrupt westernization. The favourite slur of an Islamist against a woman is that she's "too much of a feminist." This sexist Islamist ideology has firmly taken root in North America and is bent upon silencing the voices of reason and moderation. And their main tactic is to entrap Muslim women in oppressive debates about dress codes and keep them away from knowledge and practice of their own God-given rights. The mosque has become a men's club where women are not welcome except in the basement or if they're making tea in the kitchen for the men.

But this cannot last. I take strength and inspiration in the fact that with support for the moderate voices in Islam and with more understanding about who we are, there will be positive change both within and around us. In Morocco and Malaysia, women have brought about landmark changes in divorce laws. In Saudi Arabia, women have bravely broken the law against female driving. The silent gender jihad revolution continues and it is overcoming Islamism. This will be one of the most important things that brings about change from within.

H

Hate

I was once asked by an interviewer about how radicalization takes place among certain Muslims. The answer is hate. I explained that hate is the trigger that allows the radical to dehumanize others and justifies violence against them. Research into the dangers of radical jihadist ideology shows us that hate is the most potent tool in radicalizing Muslims. When we think of the spread of such hatred, we imagine radical madrassahs in the Afghan tribal lands, or Ayatollahs' sermons, or YouTube videos from the Islamic State. But radicalizing hatred can be spread much more subtly than that. Like at conferences, in the West, hosted by the same Muslims you might see on a CNN panel show.

In 2012, the Islamic Circle of North America hosted a conference called "Carry the Light" in Toronto.[11] With a name like that, it hardly sounds hateful. And the website advertisement for it made it sound positively caring: "The purpose of this convention is to provide avenues for the Muslim Community in Canada for personal excellence in faith, worship and morality. It is also a platform to share the basis for moral,

---

11   *Islamic Circle of North America – Canada, "Carry the Light Convention.*

social and economic development of Canada with Canadian society at large." How sweet.

But then I looked at the list of speakers invited to this conference. Their background and history do not support "personal excellence or morality" as I understand them. They have a history of making homophobic, anti-Semitic and misogynist remarks. And this is the most insidious way that Islamists spread hatred against the West and against anyone who does not subscribe to their political fundamentalism.

There was Linda Sarsour, an American political activist and former executive director of the Arab American Association of New York. In a conference hosted by the Islamic Society of North America, Sarsour said that American Muslims should not humanize Israelis and warned against normalization or friendly relations with Israelis: "If you're on the side of the oppressor, or you're defending the oppressor, or you're actually trying to humanize the oppressor, then that's a problem sisters and brothers, and we got to be able to say: that is not the position of the Muslim American community." This is what dehumanization means.[12] The same goes for her comments about famous critics of Islam, Ayaan Hirsi Ali and Brigitte Gabriel. About them, Sarsour said, " I wish I could take their vaginas away — they don't deserve to be women."

Two other speakers, Boonaa Mohammed and Ustadh AbdelRahman Murphy, had also publicly made anti-Semitic remarks. Murphy has dehumanized Jews in Israel by stating there is "no such thing as an innocent Israeli," works for an institute that warns Muslims who want to be pure not to "not resemble the Jews," and suggests that Jews are "impure" and "unclean." Mohammed has talked of "the evil Zionist control over media and foreign affairs" and accuses Israel of "killing innocent Muslims," while likening the Israeli people to Nazis.

Also on the bill was Imam Siraj Wahhaj, the African-American imam of Al-Taqwa Mosque in Brooklyn and the leader of the Muslim Alliance in North America. He was also the former

---

12   *Gary Willig, "Linda Sarsour: Muslims should not 'humanize' Israelis," Israel National News, September 9, 2018.*

vice-president of the Islamic Society of North America. Wahhaj was identified by U.S. prosecutors as an unindicted co-conspirator in the 1993 World Trade Center bombing, and was a character witness in the trial of Omar Abdel-Rahman, or the "Blind Sheik," who was convicted of that attempted attack. At that time, Wahhaj described the Blind Sheik as a "respected scholar" and "strong preacher of Islam."[13]

He has also denounced "lesbianism and homosexuality" and condemned North American laws for not forbidding "fornication and adultery." And he supports Sharia punishments, like stoning and the cutting off of limbs.

And there was Lord Nazir Ahmed of Rotherham,[14] the member of the House of Lords who was suspended for blaming a Jewish conspiracy for his imprisonment for dangerous driving. He was texting and driving when he killed someone with his Jaguar, but he blamed his conviction and sentence on the Jews because they "own newspapers and TV channels."

When he learned that the U.S. was putting a US$10 million bounty on the Pakistani terror leader Hafiz Saeed for planning the 2008 Mumbai terror attacks that killed 164 innocent people, Ahmed suggested[15] he would offer a multimillion-pound bounty for U.S. presidents George W. Bush and Barack Obama.

ICNA had the nerve to claim that this convention was aimed at inspiring Muslims to implement the true spirit of Islam in their lives and invite others towards the universal message of Islam. As an observant Muslim, I can assure you that promoting hate and anti-Semitism is definitely not the true spirit of Islam. It is the spirit of radical Islamists, who use Islam as a cover to dehumanize Jews and westerners, as well as

---

13   *"Siraj Wahhaj, controversial New York imam to speak at same conference as Linda Sarsour in Toronto." Centre for Investigative Research Canada, Setepmber 24, 2018.*

14   *Jonny Paul, "British MP blames prison term on Jewish conspiracy," The Jerusalem Post, March 14, 2013.*

15   *"Muslim Peer's 10m to capture Obama was actually a legal fund to put Obama on trial," Daily Mail UK, April 16 2012.*

non-Muslim minorities in Muslim countries, as a radicalization tool. And they are spreading that hate right under our noses, ironically in the name of "personal excellence in faith, worship and morality."

Honour Killings

On January 29, 2012, the Ontario Superior Court imposed mandatory sentences of life in prison with no chance of parole for 25 years, on Mohammad Shafia, his second wife Tooba Yahya, and their son Hamed Shafia. The polygamous Shafia family had come to Canada from Afghanistan. The three were found guilty by a jury of four counts of first-degree murder for drowning Shafia's three daughters, Zainab, 19, Sahar, 17 and Geeti, 13, as well as Shafia's older wife, Rona Amir Mohammed. After drowning the sisters and the other, childless wife, Shafia and the other murderers stuffed them into a car and pushed it into the Rideau Canal in Kingston, Ontario to make it look like an accident.[16]

In delivering the three life sentences, Ontario Judge Robert Maranger emphasized the vile factor that it was "honour" that had motivated the killing. The controlling, domineering and abusive Mohammad Shafia had believed that his teen girls were too westernized, dressing too immodestly, and were fraternizing with boys, and so dishonouring his family's name, and that his first wife was too tolerant of it. "The apparent reason behind these cold-blooded, shameful murders was that the four completely innocent victims offended your twisted notion of honour," said Justice Maranger. "A notion of honour that is founded upon the domination and control of women, a sick notion of honour that has absolutely no place in any civilized society."

The details of the case turned into a debate among Canadian Muslims over whether the crime really was a so-called "honour killing,"

---

16   *Michael Friscolanti, "Inside the Shafia killings that shocked a nation," Maclean's, March 3, 2016.*

rather than focusing on the unspeakable suffering and deaths of the victims. Some Muslims rejected the idea, calling it a matter of "domestic violence" or trouble with teenagers. Let us be clear: Domestic violence is abominable, and so-called honour murders are the most dreadful form of domestic violence. Neither should be permitted in any society or within Islam.

But in the wake of the Shafia murders, few Canadian Muslims addressed any means to protect Muslim women from honour-based violence, which is far more common in Muslim families than many people want to admit. And while it is most widely practiced in places like Afghanistan, Pakistan, Kurdistan, Saudi Arabia, and other Islamic countries, there is no country where it doesn't touch at least some Muslim families. Yet to some Muslims, it seemed as if the alleged honour of the homicidal, fanatical father was actually more important than the lives of his children and his wife. There were, incredibly, even those who sympathized with the words of the murderous Mohammad Shafia that were captured by police wiretaps during their investigation of the murder, when he said, "This is my word to you: Be I dead or alive, nothing in the world is above your honour... I am telling you now and I was telling you before that whoever play(s) with my honour, my words are the same... There is no value of life without honour."

No doubt the influence that the misogyny perpetuated by Islamism has corrupted the ability among some Muslims to see the horror of the murder against these women and girls. Many Muslims believe, like Shafia, that there is no value of life without honour. And yet there is no question that this belief is in absolute contrast with Islamic law. When it comes to murder, the Qur'an follows explicitly the judgment of Jewish law in prohibiting killing except for those guilty of a capital crime. The Qur'an states in verse ("aya") 5:32, that God "dictated to the House of Israel that whoever kills a soul unless in retaliation for a killing or corruption of the people — it is as if the murderer had killed all of humanity. And whoever saves one from death — it is as if the person saved all of humanity." On this, Jewish and Muslim law agree: The value of one life is the same as that as the value of all the lives of humanity.

So-called honour killings appear to have begun in Afghan and Kurdish Sunni Muslim before the arrival of Islam. And yet, even after Islamization, these killings not only persist, they have taken root among Muslims in the Middle East. Muslim clerics have failed appallingly in their religious duty to prevent them.

Among South Asians living in the West, honour violence often targets young women who show independence rather than conform to retrograde customs, rules, and oversight, as in the Shafia case. In these cases, the men are convinced they are guardians of women's virtue, and are obliged to control their wives, daughters, and even their mothers to enforce the "code of honour." (There is a clear similarity, here, to members of gangs of who kill because they feel "disrespected.")

Muslim women caught in this paradigm of this stagnant pseudo-morality may first be warned, then attacked, with acid thrown in their faces or other mutilations, before they are finally killed. The Shafia murder trial heard how he beat his teen daughters, sometimes with the help of his son, for coming home late from the mall, among other minor infractions. This twisted sense of honour may induce family members to conspire, as in the Shafia case, to commit these crimes together, because honour is defined by the group. The same logic that sees a daughter as "dishonouring" her family, is the same logic that motivates a family to plan her murder.

In fact, in some countries, so-called honour murders are not stigmatized at all. The perpetrators are acclaimed as heroes for defending their families. Even the Royal Jordanian Penal Code provides a free pass for this terrible violence against women, stating that "he who discovers his wife or one of his female relatives committing adultery and kills, wounds, or injures one of them, is exempted from any penalty." And so these killings go on…and on. And the toll of violence is staggering.

According to a United Nations report, 4,000 women were killed in Pakistan in the name of honour between 1998 and 2003. In a study of female deaths in Alexandria, Egypt, 4%7 of the women were killed by a relative after the woman had been raped, which is considered to shame the family. In Jordan and Lebanon, 70 to 75%of the perpetrators of so-called honour murders are the women's brothers.

Muslims need to deal with this blot on our faith that is only made worse by the sexism that Islamism encourages among Muslim men, by devaluing female lives. Communities must educate male leaders about respecting equal rights for women within the religion as well as obeying the guarantees in the constitutions of many countries. Muslim communities must provide education to women about their rights and provide help for those who need to flee honour-based violence. And western governments must make clear that immigrants who come here respect the rights of women and children. The Prophet Muhammed himself had instructed emigrants to non-Muslim lands that a Muslim in a non-Muslim country must obey the laws and customs of his new country. That is another Islamic teaching that clearly too many honour-obsessed Muslims are choosing to ignore.

I

Islamism in History

The modern rise of Islamism is repeating a history that Muslims have experienced before.

In the year 661, Muawiyah, a governor of Syria and an opponent of the Prophet Muhammed, became the ruler of the Umayyad Caliphate, which spanned from Cordoba across Northern Africa and the Middle East, after taking power from the Prophet's grandson. Muawiyah was a known tyrant and ruled by force. And he was the originator of Islamism — because he valued Islam not as a faith, but used it as a political force for expansion and used its power to oppress minorities and other Muslims who challenged him. He used it to deny people basic human rights. Freedom of speech was crushed. The people were subjugated to his rule. It was a precursor to the sort of Islamism we see practiced today in Iran, Saudi Arabia and other Muslim lands.

It didn't have to be this way. Ira M. Lapidus, professor emeritus of Middle Eastern and Islamic history at the University of California, Berkeley, notes that by the 10th century, some governments in the Muslim world were liberal-minded. They had developed an effective separation of mosque and state, as political control passed from Muslim leaders "into the hands of generals, administrators, governors, and local provincial lords; the Caliphs had lost all effective political power."

But Islamism does not tolerate such separation. Because Islamism is about power. Islamists are pathologically obsessed with power.

Indonesia is the largest Muslim country on earth, and minorities used to thrive there. For decades, political Islam was suppressed, and the state promoted "Pancasila" — the unity of all beliefs under God, without privileging Islam —as the foundational philosophy of the Indonesian state. But Islamists there are gaining power. In 2019, Islamists in Indonesia rioted for two days after their presidential candidate came within 10%of winning power, claiming the election had been rigged. But to stay in power, President Joko Widodo has had to ally with other hardline Islamists. The governor of Jakarta, a Christian, was jailed in 2016 for nearly two years after he was accused of insulting the Qur'an. Police persecution of LGBT people is on a dramatic rise. And there are growing calls for Sharia law to be made official across the country.

The founder of modern Turkey, Mustafa Kemal Ataturk, turned the city's Hagia Sophia mosque into a museum in 1935, after the Ottomans had seized it from Christians in the 15th century and converted what had been the largest Christian cathedral in the world for nearly 1,000 years. This year, Turkish President Recep Tayyip Erdogan declared that the Hagia Sophia would again become a mosque. Erdogan is a would-be caliph. A strongman in the mould of Muawiyah. He has upended Ataturk's secular state and replaced it with Islamic rule. Islamists have no interest in tolerant, liberal government. They use Islam to consolidate their power.

In a brilliant 2015 essay in Newsweek titled "A Short History of Islamism," Robin Wright of the Woodrow Wilson Institute explains that Islamists today take many forms. From the comparatively "moderate" sort, such as Erdogan, to the most extreme variety, such as those in the Islamic State. But there is no question that Islamists, as a group, are more visible than ever, more brazen than ever, and are, once again, on the march.

"In 1992, after a decade underground, Hezbollah's Hassan Nasrallah led the Shiite party into Lebanese elections," Wright explains. "Egypt's Muslim Brotherhood ran for parliament in 1995, after a decade of competing under cover of other political parties. Jordan's Islamic Action Front became the largest opposition party elected to parliament. From scenic Morocco and sleepy Kuwait to teeming Yemen, Islamist parties captured the imagination of many voters. "

Iran, along with Qatar and Turkey, are leading the charge in pushing Islamism's worldwide spread, funding organizations and individuals to promote their subversive ideology. And, worryingly, they have a receptive audience waiting for them. According to Clarion Project's short documentary By the Numbers, the mindset of a majority of Muslims favours Islamist ideology. But while they may not all be violent right now, both ancient and modern history tell us that it does not take long for Islamists to resort to terror and violence to achieve their goals, pushing aside the faith of Islam and using political Islam to advance a reign of brutal power.

Islamophobia

Islamophobia has almost become an obsession for a certain group of academics, politicians and Muslims across North America.

In Canada, the House of Commons passed Motion M-103 in 2017 that "condemns Islamophobia" and calls on the government to "recognize the need to quell the increasing public climate of hate and fear" through a "whole-of-government approach." Also mentioned are other "forms of systemic racism and religious discrimination," but only Islamophobia is mentioned by name. The government then released a new three-year anti-racism strategy responding to M-103, that includes a definition of Islamophobia taken from the Ontario

Human Rights Commission, which reads: "(Islamophobia includes) racism, stereotypes, prejudice, fear or acts of hostility directed towards individual Muslims or followers of Islam in general. In addition to individual acts of intolerance and racial profiling, Islamophobia can lead to viewing and treating Muslims as a greater security threat on an institutional, systemic and societal level."

Some have compared it to Canada's own blasphemy law, given that this country once prized the principle of free speech, even for opinions that might offend certain groups. And Canadians are understandably worried this prevents them from asking simple and valid questions about Islam, fundamentalism, Islamist radicalization and terrorism.

In the U.K., politicians have been trying to follow suit, with the All-Party Parliamentary Group on British Muslims proposing their own blasphemy laws, by trying to get Parliament to adopt a similar definition of Islamophobia as "rooted in racism and is a type of racism that targets expressions of Muslimness or perceived Muslimness," which has been adopted by the Labour Party, the Liberal Democratic Party, the Welsh independence party Plaid Cymru, the mayor of London and several local councils. U.K. Conservative MP Nusrat Ghani, herself a Muslim, warned that even though bigotry against Muslims did exist, the government must be careful not to make speech-stifling blasphemy laws that accord with the agenda of extremists. "One is focusing on the victims of anti-Muslim hate or abuse," she said. "And (another) is ensuring that we continue to have the freedom of speech to criticize Islam, as you would criticize any religion, and also criticize extremists within Islam, because if they had their way, I wouldn't be here sitting at the top table speaking to you."

Meanwhile, the OIC flaunts its "Islamophobia Observatory," and has long been pushing for international legislation against what it considers Islamophobia. In 2018, Pakistan reportedly[17] tried to organize the OIC to make an international convention against speech insulting to Muslims into part of a "migration pact." Pakistani Prime

---

17   *Danielle Smith, "UN migration pact part of the plan to extinguish Canadian identity," Global News, December 4, 2018.'*

Minister Imran Khan then met with Pakistan, Turkey and Malaysia at the UN[18] to plan an English-language Islamic television channel to broadcast against Islamophobia.

What is ironic and hypocritical about all the Islamophobia hype by members of the OIC is their double standard when it comes to minorities in their own lands. Saudi Arabia, Pakistan, Egypt, Turkey, Mauritania, Nigeria, Sudan, Bangladesh, Iraq, Kuwait, Syria, the Palestinian Authority and Iran are all among the OIC members that have committed appalling human rights violations against minorities.

And then there is the endless parade of conferences around the world, ceaseless flogging alarm over Islamophobia. In one recent year alone, I counted "Islam, Political Islam, and Islamophobia: an International Conference" and "Islam, Politics and Islamophobia" in Indiana; the "Women in Islam: Eradicating Islamophobia" conference in Atlanta; and "The International Conference on Islamophobia" in Istanbul, which claimed in its promotional materials that "the groundless fear and intolerance of Islam and Muslims, has swept the world." In Berkeley, California there has been an Islamophobia conference every year for the past decade!

I guess it's no surprise, then, that at the university there, there is an ongoing "Islamophobia Research and Documentation Project" led by a professor who teaches an entire course focused on Islamophobia, in which he has assigned his students to go on Twitter and tweet out victimhood narratives about Muslims.

Of course, anti-Muslim hatred and bigotry is real. It's properly called xenophobia, and it is abhorrent, the same way that hatred and bigotry against any other broad community is abhorrent. And yes, it needs to be addressed. However, there are already laws in Canada, the U.S. and the U.K. that protect individuals against attacks and unlawful discrimination on the basis of their religion. And despite the incredible amount of space that Islamophobia obsessives take up, statistics show that they are hardly the only ones who face racism and bigotry: hate

18   *PTI, "Pakistan, Turkey, Malaysia to jointly launch Islamic TV channel: PM Imran Khan," The Hindu, September 26, 2018.*

crimes are highest against Jews, followed by LGBT people, then Blacks, and then Muslims.

So, let's take a real, honest look at this idea of supposedly growing and widespread Islamophobia. According to a 1997 report by the U.K.'s Runnymede Trust, the term has existed since the 1980s and was first used in print in 1991. Runnymede defined Islamophobia as referring to "dread or hatred of Islam — and, therefore, to the fear or dislike of all Muslims," adding that "within Britain it means that Muslims are frequently excluded from the economic, social and public life of the nation… and are frequently victims of discrimination and harassment."

Are the majority of Muslims really excluded from the economic, social and public life of western nations? There are no statistics to verify such a statement. To the contrary, most North American Muslims live with full freedoms, unless they ghettoize themselves by choice, and many do.

So how did this Islamophobia theory become mainstream and so popular? In North America there is already an existing sense of guilt, which Christians have prebuilt into their faith. North Americans feel additional guilt over their countries' past treatment of Aboriginals or immigrants. Europeans have guilt about colonization and the Holocaust. And Islamists readily and eagerly build on this guilt, playing the victimhood card to maximum effect, with the help of sympathetic academics, activists and political leaders, building it into a highly profitable Islamophobia industry that helps divert attention away from their more radical activities, like pushing Sharia law, the caliphate, and radicalization.

Islamophobia is also a convenient pseudo-cause around which to whip up young followers: they are informed, whether true or not, that they have much to be aggrieved about and that the only solution is to close down free speech, demonize all who might have an opinion that differs from theirs or ask uncomfortable questions, and to build authoritarian political movements where young people feel they can meaningfully participate.

But in the long run it can only numb the minds and hearts of young Muslims growing up in the West, and destroy all spirit of enquiry and independent thinking. That's one of its objectives. Today, many Muslims in the West use "Islamophobia" as a penalty card against free speech whenever there is criticism of Muslims. It's a kneejerk and reactionary response that immediately stifles the sort of dialogue, debate and discussion that are necessary in a healthy, thriving democracy. And that's exactly what they mean it to do.

J

Jihad

"Struggle against oppression, terrorism and tyranny" in the Arabic language is called "jihad." Scholars of the Qur'an tell us the verses dealing with this topic are specific and not intended to imply a general meaning for just anyone to decide to go around attacking non-Muslims. As a matter of fact, the Qur'an addresses Jews and Christians as people of the book and refers to them many times. In some places in the Qur'an, God chastises the Jews for abandoning the Sabbath and admonishes Christians for their belief that Jesus is the son of God, although God does affirm that Jesus is indeed a prophet in a line of prophets. Indeed, Jesus is mentioned in the Qur'an more times than Muhammad is.

There is no injunction in the Qur'an to kill others. When killing is mentioned in the Qur'an, it happens in a historical context. After being driven out of their homes and turned out into the desert to starve, Allah allowed Muslims — after years of trying to make peace with their enemies — to fight to win back Mecca. But only within very specific limitations.

Rules of war are clearly indicated in the Qur'an. Fighters are not to harm non-combatants, people in worship, places of worship, women and children or the environment. Those who misuse the word jihad today as an excuse to slaughter Jews, Christians, Hindus and other so-called infidels, ignore the Qur'an, Surah v:27-35. "Because of this, we decreed for the Children of Israel that anyone who murders any person who had not committed murder or horrendous crimes, it shall be as if he murdered all the people..."

One reason for the misinterpretation of the Qur'an is because the early rulers, after the death of the Prophet, politicized the faith and used carefully chosen verses to promote their own political agendas. When the faith is politicized, its spiritual message is degraded. Jihad today is an attempt by Islamists to promote 7th century laws in the 21st century. If early digital computers, made less than 100 years ago would not be compatible with our needs today, then laws of jihad from 1,400 years ago certainly aren't either. Those who use them to justify violence have no interest in the legitimacy of the laws. They just want violence.

K

Kids Being Radicalized

According to the UN, there are more than 250,000 child soldiers fighting around the world in more than 20 different conflicts. The Combating Terrorism Center reports that ISIS had more than 1,500 kids on the front lines and trained 1,000 more to become suicide bombers in the first six months of 2015.

Child radicalization is a horror on a global scale. The problem has spread from the child soldiers on the front lines to the living rooms of Europe and North America. Radicalization has become easier for extremists through the Internet, the new weapon being brandished by Islamist terrorists in accordance with the mandate of the Muslim Brotherhood to "weaken the West from within." Children as young as three are watching these videos on YouTube. One Palestinian video available online shows Farfur[19] the Mouse being "martyred" while fighting the "criminal, plundering Jews."

---

19   *"The Fall of Farfur," YouTube Video, 4:41, posted by amplifier515, July 7, 2007*

CNN reported that in 2018, about 1,000 investigations of connections with ISIS were open in all 50 states. In August 2018, 11 children were found in a compound in New Mexico being trained by an American radical Islamist to commit school shootings. In June 2019, a 22-year-old Bangladeshi living in New York was arrested for plotting an attack on Times Square. In Minneapolis, 45 boys and young men have left the local Somali community to join al-Shabab or ISIS. Dozens more were stopped before they could leave.

These are only a part of the statistics that tell us we are facing a huge crisis; very few people are willing to speak about the dangers of the radicalization of youths.

In 2019, leaders and experts with the Clarion Project gathered in Washington, D.C. to hold an exclusive pre-release Congressional screening of the documentary, *Kids Chasing Paradise.* The organization flew in key experts and other leaders around the world who are fighting against radical extremism and who are affiliated with the film to educate Congress, hold media briefings and present the program, Prevent Violent Extremism, at the National Press Club.

Kids Chasing Paradise tells the incredible story of ordinary people who have been directly affected by this radicalization and are now trying to prevent it from happening to others. In addition to some in-depth coverage of youths being taught hate, violence and radicalization, the film features:

- Christianne Boudreau, a Canadian mother whose son, Damian, was killed while fighting for ISIS. She now co-ordinates the Mothers for Life Network, which brings together mothers of radicalized jihadis to support one another and combat radicalization.

- Tania Joya, a former extremist who is now working out of Texas on deradicalization. Her ex-husband was radicalized in Texas as a teenager and became ISIS's main propagandist in Syria. Joya admits she actually once wanted her children to grow up to be jihadists. Now she embraces human rights and western values.

- Nicola Benyahia, a British woman who founded Families for Life, a non-profit organization focused on deradicalization and support for families of young extremists. When her son Rasheed joined ISIS, she found support in Christianne Boudreau and they started both a professional collaboration and personal friendship

The movie is accompanied by a workshop called "Preventing Violent Extremism," based on the concept that no one is born a terrorist or extremist. It is a primary goal of Islamists to manipulate people into being radicalized, and children and young people are the most easily manipulated of all.

L

Local Islamist Politics

If you thought Islamist political parties looking to promote Sharia law were something that just existed in the Middle East and Africa, then you haven't been paying close enough attention to the local scene right here in Canada.

The Islamic Party of Ontario is offering itself as the solution to all problems plaguing Canada, the same way Hezbollah offers itself as the solution to all problems plaguing Lebanon. In fact, a more accurate name for this disturbing Canadian political party would be the Islamist Party. It certainly doesn't deserve to call itself an Islamic party, since it clearly does not represent anyone but the most extreme fundamentalists of my faith. And yet it's working to win power, right here in our own backyard.[20]

Reading like a Sharia instruction manual, the website of the Islamic Party of Ontario is written in a framework that's difficult to challenge legally. No matter how colourfully this manifesto is wrapped

---

20   *Islamic Party of Ontario*

in the cloak of the Canadian Charter of Rights and Freedoms, make no mistake about it: Its premise is entirely Islamist in flavour and has no silver lining.

Among other things, the website declares:

- *We understand and believe that Islam is the native "Deen" of Ontario and Canada. (That means they think that Islam is the natural religion, custom and justice system for Canada.)*

- *The relationship established under a marriage contract is a sacred union between a man and a woman. God made Adam and Eve — not Adam and Steve. (No minced words here: They have no tolerance for LGBTQ rights.)*

- *We believe in a complete ban on abortion except in a situation when a mother's life is in danger.*

- *Liquor, drugs, adultery, gambling, etc. should be banned in society.*

- *The experience and surveys show that "boy only" and "girl only" schools produce much better results. We will support the gradual transition from co-education to gender-specific schools.*

Although I would never support this so-called Islamic party, some Muslims might rally to it simply because of its name. If I were them, I would ask these questions first:

- Is this party going to include all 72 sects of Islam?

- Will it allow anyone who is from one of the Muslim groups that Sunni Muslims consider to be impure and not true Muslims, like the Ahmaddiya?

- Which of the five schools of Islamic thought is it pursuing?

When I immigrated to Canada, I thought I was coming to a society that properly separated religion and state. That's why a lot of immigrants — particularly Muslim immigrants — come here. Here are just some of the countries that are run by a government based on religion: Saudi Arabia, Iran, Pakistan and Afghanistan. All these countries have gross human rights violations because religion is misused. Women's rights are almost non-existent, and minorities are persecuted. Most countries run this way are failed states, because human rights are seen through the lens of religion instead of the other way around.

The Islamic Party of Ontario may be naive in thinking it will move ahead. Perhaps it has not taken into account Canadians' ability to think with reason and logic, and their unequivocal embrace of freedoms. It's not hard for any Canadian — Muslim or non-Muslim — to see that the agenda of this new Islamic party is really about promoting Islamism, to make Canada less free. Hopefully the manifesto of this religious party crumbles before it even has a chance to solidify.

M

M-103

On Dec. 5, 2016, Canadian MP Iqra Khalid proposed a parliamentary motion against Islamophobia, called Motion 103. M-103 singles out Islam for special protection. It "condemns Islamophobia" and calls on the government to "recognize the need to quell the increasing public climate of hate and fear" through a "whole-of-government approach." Mentioned only vaguely are "all forms of systemic racism and religious discrimination," but only Islamophobia is mentioned by name.

Khalid began her statement to the House of Commons by saying, "Mr. Speaker, I am a young, brown, Muslim, Canadian woman ..."

I find it curious that Khalid begins by identifying herself first as brown, then Muslim and lastly as a Canadian. The way I see it, a Canadian member of Parliament should identify as Canadian first. And being Canadian means showing concern for everyone, not just a select group of people.

Perhaps Khalid has not studied what Islamophobia really mean. It would be more troubling if she knew full well that the term

"Islamophobia" is a tool used by the Muslim Brotherhood and other Islamist groups as a way to "play victim" for the purpose of silencing critics of Islamism. It is also in sync with a constant push by the OIC to internationally ban any criticism of Islam or Muslims as blasphemy.

As a Canadian Muslim, I am very concerned about the direction in which we are headed. My family and I came to Canada 30 years ago to embrace the values of a liberal democracy, of which freedom of speech is the most vital.

M-103, which was passed by the House of Commons in 2017, was meant to kill free speech and goes directly against Canadian values. Canadians must speak out against this attack on their democratic values. But now they won't, because they are being silenced by the fear of being called Islamophobes.

M-103 will only increase the frustration of ordinary Canadian who want (and have the right) to ask questions regarding Islam. Being concerned about creeping Sharia is not "Islamophobic." Criticizing honour-based violence and female genital mutilation is not "Islamophobic." Speaking out against radicalization and its connection to terrorism is also not "Islamophobic."

I was one of several people who testified against M-103 to the House of Commons standing committee on Canadian Heritage. Here is a transcript of my remarks:

M-103 TESTIMONY

Standing Committee on Canadian Heritage

42nd. Parliament, Wednesday Sept. 27, 2017 — M-103

Raheel Raza, President, Council for Muslims Facing Tomorrow

Madam Chairman, members of the committee, ladies and gentlemen, thank you for the opportunity to address this committee.

My name is Raheel Raza and I am president of the Council for Muslims Facing Tomorrow. My family and I will have been in Canada for 30 years next year. Like most immigrants we came here to embrace democracy, gender equality and freedom of speech.

I can say with conviction that Canada is the best country in the world, with a role to play in terms of leadership, and I thank God for being a Canadian citizen to share in its values.

Today we are here to discuss Motion 103.

Let me make it abundantly clear that bigotry, hate and racism have to be condemned in the strongest terms. Sadly, they have always been an integral part of human civilization. But human dignity depends upon our unequivocal condemnation of these ugly values and we *must* speak out against them.

Having said this, we are entrapped by use of the term "Islamophobia" which is not clearly defined. As I read the text of Motion 103, I can agree with the overall intent, but only without use of this term, because Islamophobia can and has been used to confuse the masses and stifle free speech.

I've just returned from attending the 36th session of UNHRC (UN Human Rights Committee) in Geneva and have seen how the Organization of Islamic Co-operation has for years been working towards stemming any critique of religion. Critique of religion, by the way, is not critique of people. If there are aspects of any faith that are veering towards human rights infractions, they must be discussed and debated. Religion is an idea and ideas don't have rights — people do.

Canada should therefore be concerned about the rights of all its peoples and not allow itself to fall into the traps laid out by vested agendas.

Right now the world is screaming for an Islamic reform to welcome Muslims into the 21st century, by a fresh wave of ideas through the lens of modernity and free thinking keeping human rights in the forefront.

This is not entirely a new phenomenon. Because in the 9th century there was a large community of Muslims known as free thinkers who would debate and discuss all aspects of faith to come to a logical conclusion. The ruling elite found this to be a threat and over a period of time, one by one, they were eliminated. This silencing of all debate and discussion in Islam has put us Muslims in a ridiculous position. It also puts a target on the backs of those who want change.

Reform has taken place in other faiths as well. Christians will celebrate 500 years of their reform this year. How does reform happen? It takes place through reflection using reason and logic and yes, a healthy critique. Without constructive criticism, no faith can grow and develop.

As an observant Muslim, I don't believe I have to be the caretaker or defender of my faith.

However, the word most synonymous with Muslim these days is terrorism. Do I want to leave this as legacy for my children and grandchildren? Absolutely not! As such, Muslim communities have to do most of the heavy lifting in shunning or abandoning negative practices that have crept into our faith and culture. Such as FGM (female genital mutilation), forced and underage marriage, slavery, polygamy, armed violence against civilians disguised as jihad, forceful imposition of Sharia laws, and preaching of hate and intolerance towards minorities.

It's through this reform that major changes have taken place in Muslim communities.

For example:

- In India the supreme court has banned a centuries-old Islamic tradition of a man saying "I divorce you" thrice and it was automatically granted.

- Women in Morocco helped change the polygamy laws.

- In Tunisia, a landmark decision was made allowing Muslim women to marry non-Muslim men, which according to Sharia laws is not acceptable.

- Bangladesh has altered its constitution from Islamic to secular.

- The House of Lords in the U.K. is debating and challenging certain practices of Sharia courts.

My point is that Canada, with its thriving Muslim population, should be a leading voice in encouraging such reforms, rather than encouraging them to hide behind a motion to curtail free speech.

As well, in a secular country (which we strive for), the state should have no business in religious matters.

M-103 as it stands, with usage of the term Islamophobia, has divided Canadians into "us" and "them." By singling out one faith community in this motion, it seems that Islam and Muslims are exclusive and demand special attention. When in actual fact, statistics show us that hate crimes against the Jews, Blacks and LGBTQ communities are the highest. Polls show that more than 70 per cent of Canadians don't agree with Motion 103.

As for Muslims, let's see how badly they are really treated. There are approximately over 100 Mosques and 50 Islamic Organizations just in the Greater Toronto Area. There are 11 Muslim MPs in our government and Muslim prayers are taking place in some public schools. This doesn't look like systemic racism to me!

However, there are cases of bigotry and racism, so I encourage this committee to strengthen the laws to curb hatred and discrimination against all Canadians — not just one section.

Thank you.

Multiculturalism

Canada likes to boast about its multiculturalism. There's a "Canadian Multiculturalism Day" every June, although no one except the government seems to mark it. In 2019, the prime minister, Justin Trudeau, issued a statement that crowed about how wonderfully multicultural Canada is, while, in his trademark style, lecturing Canadians about how they're still not politically correct enough. "We must all continue to learn about each other, embrace our diversity, and celebrate what it is to be Canadian — while learning from the mistakes in our past, and making sure never to repeat them," he said. "We are also not immune to the violent and hateful extremism unfolding around the world. By calling out and standing up to divisive speech and acts, we put ourselves forward as an example — as people who treat each other with respect, champion the rights of all, and embrace diversity as a strength."

This is the exactly wrong way of looking at multiculturalism. It defines it as feeling guilty for Canada's history and shame for the way Canada is today. This is the kind of approach to multiculturalism that Islamists can use as a fertile ground for their incessant claims of Islamophobia, and their ever-increasing demands for accommodation of practices and attitudes that are at odds with Canadian values and society.

In 2011, I was lucky enough to travel to Australia. And I saw first-hand how multiculturalism should be — and could be, in Canada, if we only stood up to the shaming and guilt that are being used to manipulate us.

I was invited to Adelaide by the Association of Heads of Independent Schools of Australia, to address school principals from across the country about cultural diversity in schools — its strengths and challenges. I drew from my experience with Canadian schools, where I find teachers are rather confused about how to deal with diversity because they're getting mixed messages. A prime example: Many schools are not allowed to make Christmas a schoolwide celebration, while festivals of other faiths are highlighted. Similarly, the Lord's Prayer has been nixed in Canadian public schools while other prayers are given special accommodation.

I was pleasantly surprised to hear that in Australia, many principals can make independent decisions on how to deal with multi-ethnic, multifaith issues. Most of the schools are Catholic or Anglican and some principals told me that they inform immigrant parents, as soon as they come for admission, what they can expect in these schools, so they're not caught off guard by mixed-gender classrooms, Christian education and chapel. Parents then have a choice to accept the rules or find another school. (In some cases, special accommodations are made for individual non-Christian children, but that's up to individual schools and there are no school-wide policies.)

Despite the diversity of students, including Aboriginals and immigrants, there were fewer problems with multiculturalism in Australian schools than I've encountered in schools elsewhere, and educators are much more pragmatic about dealing with issues. Crucially, they draw a distinct line between reasonable and unreasonable accommodation.

While I was in Australia, I also travelled to Sydney as a guest of Ida Lichter, a psychologist and author of the book Muslim Women Reformers. She arranged for me to speak at the Sydney Institute on the topic of creeping Sharia in the West. I had explained the difference between Sharia as a moral and ethical guideline and Sharia as it's become today in most Muslim societies; that is, a manmade law, and a tool for Islamists.

I was impressed at how well-informed the audience was, but also how open they were to discussing what in Canada would be an off-limits topic, and discussing it in a very non-politically correct way. We had a respectful dialogue, including a critique of Islamists' efforts to impose religion in the public realm, demands for a two-tier legal system and excessive accommodation in the name of religious freedom.

My Australian audience were also open to solutions and didn't mind me giving them a bit of a wake-up call to be better informed about the difference between Islam and Islamism, to condemn racism and hatred unequivocally, to reject racist and violent politics of any group and to stand up for their liberty and freedom with respect and dignity.

In my mind, this attitude is prevalent Down Under because multiculturalism is not — yet — a top-down government policy, so Aussies are well aware of its insidious appeal as an excuse to push subversive agendas and to excuse human rights abuses in the name of pluralism and cultural relativism.

The government also seems to be somewhat in sync with the strengths and challenges of diversity and open immigration policies. Australia faces challenges within its own Indigenous Aboriginal population and refugees, but they are open to suggestions and reform in their current policies.

I also spoke to the Union, University and Schools Club of Sydney, where there was a mixed Christian-Jewish audience of lawyers, retired judges, businesspeople and academics. There I discussed the challenges faced by Muslim women activists, especially the lack of support we get from western feminist groups. I was delighted to find that the Aussies actually got it!

One high-profile businesswoman approached me right afterward and said, "I've already enlisted other people here and we've decided that we are going to build you a mosque for women and you're coming to the opening." Needless to say, I was dumbfounded. But it also showed me the tenacity of the Australians and that they mean business in wanting to bring about change in the name of real multiculturalism.

Before you assume that Australians are intolerant, let me tell you that I also spoke to Muslim friends who have lived there for decades, and consider it the best place on earth. I even prodded a Muslim taxi driver from Pakistan to tell me about the tales of racism and discrimination that we hear about in the media, but he couldn't. There may be one or two incidents, he said, but he told me that largely Australians believe in live and let live.

He said, "If we are honest and forthcoming with them and respect them, then they respect us. I've been here 17 years and never had a problem. But there are areas of Sydney where Muslims don't mix and want their own set of laws, so obviously there is resistance to this kind of ghettoization and I, too, am against it."

It may be hard for Canadians to believe, but when a government is not politically correct and multiculturalism is allowed to mature naturally with all its ups and downs, and not thrust down people's throats or used as a political tool, people actually learn to get along.

That's definitely an approach worth trying in Canada.

Muslim-Only Enclaves

Canada is home to a large number of ethnic communities, and it's natural that when immigrants come to a new land, they tend to congregate in areas where others like them have settled.

There are also some communities that have been marginalized in their homeland, so they tend to stick together. One example is the Ahmadiyya Muslims, who have been persecuted in Pakistan, so now they live mostly in Vaughan, Ontario, a Toronto suburb, where they are close to each other and their mosque. In their particular case, it's understandable that they feel vulnerable and tend to find security in proximity to each other.

But in 2014 came news that that residents of a community in Thornhill, Ontario, another Toronto suburb, were proposing to construct two residential high-rise buildings and 61 townhouses in a low-density neighbourhood. The proposed condos would be built on the site of the Jaffari Community Centre, on Bathurst Street, and designed to contain 377 units, primarily for Muslims.

This looks uncomfortably like another one of those "Muslim only" enclaves that are already a reality in Europe, the United Kingdom, America, where they are sometimes funded by local governments and come with a slew of problems. In Britain, where this idea for Muslim-exclusive zones first took root, followers of Anjem Chaudhry, who runs the banned militant group Islam4UK, have set up "Sharia zones" in different cities. They are already taking root in Canada.

According to Daniel Pipes of the Middle East Forum, "There exist already some 10 to 20 Muslim-only enclaves in Canada and the United States, the villages run by Muslims of the Americas, a group affiliated with the Pakistani group Jamaat ul-Fuqra." In a recent letter to the U.S. government, some progressive Muslim groups have asked for Jamaat ul-Fuqra to be labelled as a terrorist group.

The backers of this proposed new Muslim-only enclave in the Toronto area have controversial baggage of their own. The Jaffari community is part of the Shia Ithna Asheri Jamaat of Toronto, which runs the East End Madrassah, a Sunday school that uses the premises of a public school to hold its classes for Muslim children. Based on a complaint, they were previously investigated for using a curriculum that promoted hate against Jews. There is concern that the curriculum being taught at the East End Madrassah was created in Iran, although no charges were laid.[21]

When asked why he supported the building of the Muslim condo project, a member of the Jaffari community was quoted in the press saying, "My family will be close to the mosque." But if your only criteria for living in Canada and bringing up your family here is to be close to your mosque, you might as well have stayed in an Islamic country. How will the children growing up in this enclave learn to integrate into Canadian society?

The answer: They won't. And no doubt this is what the Islamist strains in these community really want. No mixing with westerners. No learning Canadian values. And better to keep these Muslim kids segregated to nurture intolerance and misunderstanding of their Canadian neighbours. Not surprisingly, studies have shown that Muslim youths who grow up in ethnic enclaves are more susceptible to being radicalized compared to those who have a chance to mix and mingle in the public space.

Another question we need to ask is whether the decisions of Muslim communities in Canada should be influenced by the politics of Iran

---

21   *Stewart Bell, "Our teachings embrace and celebrate Canadian values: Toronto Mosque condemns criticism of Islamic School." National Post, November 9, 2012.*

and Saudi Arabia, who use funding to promote an insular, intolerant approach among Muslims in the West, or should these decisions be based on our collective sense of Canadian national identity and safety? In Canada, we wisely do not allow foreign money to influence elections. And yet we allow foreign money to influence our communities, and even more worryingly, our children.

When we immigrated ago, there was no pressure to live in a Muslim enclave. We knew we were coming to a country where we have freedom of religion and where we can follow our faith anywhere and in any way we want. We wanted our kids to grow up with the Canadian values of individual freedom, gender equality and liberty, while contributing the best from their own background. The corrosive effect of foreign money from Islamist governments is turning more recent Muslim immigrants inward, away from assimilating into Canadian society. That may be the very dangerous goal of the next condo project that goes up on your block.

N

9.11

There are many lessons we did not learn from 9/11 despite the fact that the fall of the Twin Towers was a turning point in modern history. The world changed. The pain and trauma of the families of the victims remains as strong as ever. Yet today, nearly 20 years down the road, it seems we have learned very little from it when it comes to protecting ourselves from Islamist extremism.

No pressure was put on penalizing countries whose citizens were directly involved in the attack on 9/11. The majority of the hijackers were from Saudi Arabia, yet it has been business as usual with the kingdom in both the U.S. and Canada, which continues to sell arms to the Saudis.

Muslims have been allowed to position themselves as victims of 9/11. Their main reaction was whether there would be a backlash against them and the panic about "Islamophobia" was the beginning of what has become a societal obsession with political correctness and sensitivity towards Muslims. I've seen cases where even talking about 9/11 is considered insensitive to Muslims. Since 9/11, Islamists have successfully shifted the narrative away from frequently well-deserved criticisms of Muslims, instead making it nearly impossible to criticize Muslims. The 9/11 attacks have been reframed as a tragedy for Muslims rather than as a tragedy for America. And this has been used as a playbook for every Islamist terror attack ever since, with gullible politicians and media playing along.

Meanwhile, the extremist and fundamentalist ideology behind the terrorist attacks of 9/11 is alive and well and rapidly spreading even today. No government effort has been taken to challenge the ideology of radical Islam. It's been left to organizations and individuals to carry out this momentous effort. And yet those who do speak out and carry out the effort to expose the radical ideology behind 9/11 are smeared as "Muslim haters."

But there has still been no attempt to deal with the important question of whether Muslims are to blame for 9/11, or whether *Islam* is to blame. This discussion would be considered blasphemy. We may never be able to have this discussion because it leaves Muslims on the defensive and brings their supporters out to shut down all discussion. But confronting this critical question is the only way to prompt real reform. Religion is an idea that does not have rights. We should be free to critique Islam the same way we are free to critique Christianity. Only people have rights. But they don't have the right to shut down discussions of topics they find uncomfortable.

Every September 11th should be an international day of mourning, and a day when we are encouraged to talk about the atrocity that occurred that day, the ideology that committed it, and how to prevent anything like it from ever happening again. It was a world-changing event that demands to be discussed and debated. Instead, we are being encouraged, just 20 short years later, to forget all about it. Let us never forget.

Niqab

The niqab, like the burqa, is not a religious requirement under Islam. The face covering, which reveals only the eyes, is a political garment favoured by Islamists. But Muslims are to take guidance from our holy scripture the Qur'an, especially in cases where there might be human-made secondary texts that are ambiguous or contradictory.

The Qur'an clearly does *not* ask us to cover our face. In fact, whenever Muslims make their pilgrimage to Mecca, women are not allowed to cover the face. I was there; I can tell you from experience.

Since we don't have a formal priesthood in Islam, we are asked to take counsel from credible religious scholars. One such scholar, Sheikh Mohamed Tantawi, dean of al-Azhar University in Cairo, which is the highest seat of learning for Sunni Muslims, has said that face-veiling is a custom that has nothing to do with the Islamic faith or the Qur'an. He stated that this practice is widely associated with more conservative trends of Islam. In fact, he has asked students in Egypt to remove the niqab in educational institutions.

Islamists want face-coverings — for women, only of course. It is part of their extremist anti-woman obsession with control. But in fact, this extremism actually defies Islamic law. Muslims are told repeatedly in the Qur'an to keep a balance. The Qur'an describes the Muslim community as "a moderate nation" (2:143). The word "moderate" here is a translation of the Arabic word *wastan*, which means "in the middle," but it can also mean "fair" or "balanced." The Prophet Muhammad has been quoted as saying, "The best of things is what is in the middle," that is, what is being done in moderation. One of the fundamental underpinnings of Islamic law is the requirement that a just balance between the rights of individuals and the interests of the society as a whole be maintained.

A few years ago, when the niqab debate was at its height, I was on a radio show with Steve Rockwell, who calls himself an imam. He brought along a huge edition of the Qur'an and I asked him to show me where it says that the face needs to be covered. He could not, because, in terms of dress, the Qur'an asks both men and women only to dress modestly. Later, on another show, after Sheikh Tantawi and some other scholars gave fatwas (authoritative rulings) that the niqab is not an Islamic requirement, Mr. Rockwell back-pedaled and said, "Well, it's not religious but cultural."

So, let's examine the niqab issue from some cultural perspectives:

When my grandmothers migrated from India to Pakistan decades ago, they used to wear a chador — a woman's cloak — as a cultural dress. But they eventually discarded it and opted for a simple head-covering, because the chador was all enveloping, hard to manage, and impractical. Similarly, when I came to Canada, I was used to wearing a shalwar kameez (a traditional Pakistani dress), made of thin material, not at all suited to this harsh climate. It didn't take me long to change to long warm trousers to adapt to the weather. Had I insisted on my own cultural dress, I would have suffered.

That's the thing about cultures. They must adapt, evolve and change. All cultures have to, in order to thrive. And those stuck entirely in centuries-old customs are carrying excess cultural baggage. The niqab is essentially a tribal custom that has been imported into the West but does not belong here. It's a mask. It's a barrier to communication because you can't see the face of the person behind the veil. In some ways, the niqab discriminates against me. If the person under the niqab can see me, and I can't see her, we are unequal.

Driving while wearing the niqab creates a problem with peripheral vision. And, in the post-9/11 world, it is a security threat: Faces need to be seen in high-risk areas like airports. Interestingly, the embassies and consulates of Saudi Arabia and Pakistan — two countries from which the ideology of the niqab has crept into Canada — have posted notices that women who wish to have their photograph taken for their passports must show their face.

And it's an Islamic injunction, agreed on by all Islamic schools of thought, that Muslims who immigrate must abide by the laws of their new countries, as long as they are not ordered to commit a sin. Since even Muslim scholars agree (and even its supporters must admit) the niqab is an artifact of a strictly cultural context, it is no sin to remove it.

Yes, Canada is a free country. People have an absolute right to wear—or not wear—whatever they want. If they want to wear a niqab, they can wear one around the house. There are limits to how we can appear in public — you can't wander the streets naked, after all. We Muslims must show our public face and identity. If we hide this, we're being dishonest to ourselves and to Canada.

O

Omar, Ilhan

Fools in the West have been duped and brainwashed into accepting the Islamist narrative, after Islamists declared war against the West, that Muslims are always and everywhere victims.

Thanks to U.S. Representative Ilhan Omar, we now have a highly visible example we can point to. When Omar opens her mouth, this perverse victim ideology is exposed for all its nonsense.

When Omar made her outrageous remarks in 2019 about 9/11, she was parroting the deflection that has been perfected by the Muslim Brotherhood and other Islamists.

"For far too long we have lived with the discomfort of being a second-class citizen, and frankly I'm tired of it, and every single Muslim in this country should be tired of it," Omar was caught on video telling an audience at an event for the Islamist-supporting and Hamas-linked Council on American-Islamic Relations (CAIR). "CAIR was founded after 9/11 because they recognized that some people did something and that all of us were starting to lose access to our civil liberties."

She made it clear in this one short, obscene statement where she stands in terms of loyalty to the land in which she lives and was democratically elected: "Some people did something." She doesn't consider the atrocities of 9/11 to be a big deal. Just something that happened. By some people, somewhere. This is how you erase the significance of 9/11. How you encourage people to put it behind them, to forget it. To avoid confronting the hateful ideology that made 9/11 happen.

Islamists are rarely happy to hear women speak and express opinions. But for Omar, and her fellow far-left squad member in Congress, Rashida Tlaib — both promote conspiracies that other U.S. politicians are Zionist puppets, and both support the anti-Israel boycott movement — Islamists are no doubt happy to make an exception. That's because these women are spreading Islamist propaganda — and using their platforms as members of Congress to do it. They also backed the impeachment of President Donald Trump. I wonder if Omar could name one Muslim country — just one — where a woman could be elected, and then try and depose the head of state, and get away with it.

So, here's to Omar for proving my point about Islamism.

P

Persecution of Christians

When I was six years old, my Muslim parents sent me to a Catholic school in Pakistan. There, the nuns asked me if I was Catholic or Protestant and not really knowing which was which, I said Protestant because it sounded exotic. I studied catechism and learned the Lord's Prayer. Then one day, my mother came for a parent-teacher meeting and discovered that I was passing myself off as a Christian. It was no big deal. My family found it funny. I had many Christian friends with whom I attended church while they celebrated Islamic festivals with me.

Pakistan, like many Muslim countries, was up until about the 1970s a tolerant and pluralistic society, with the Christian minority enjoying a decent life, largely living in peace with the Muslim majority. Then came political Islamization and changed all that.

Since then, we've seen the strangling of freedoms for minorities and steady discrimination and violence against Christians, in Pakistan — and elsewhere. In 2019, a report by British Foreign Secretary

Jeremy Hunt[22] concluded that persecution of Christians in the Middle East has become so sweeping and brutal that it is approaching a "genocide." Millions of Middle Eastern Christians have in recent decades been discriminated against, been driven from their homes, tortured, imprisoned and killed. "The inconvenient truth," the report said, is "that the overwhelming majority (80%) of persecuted religious believers are Christians." The report highlighted similar abuses throughout Muslim countries in Southeast Asia, sub-Saharan Africa and in East Asia.

In Egypt,[23] Coptic Christians have faced attacks by radical Muslims on their villages, businesses, and homes. Coptic monks have been kidnapped and tortured. Often the police take the side of the mobs. Coptic churches have been bombed and Coptic Christians have been massacred at prayer.

In Indonesia,[24] radical Muslims have massacred Christians by the thousands. Christians have been prosecuted for blasphemy (despite Christianity being ostensibly recognized as an official religion by the state) and churches have been closed by orders of local authorities. In Iran, Christians are forced to adhere to a Sharia law they do not believe in, and Muslim converts to Christianity and other Christians have been prosecuted for blasphemy. Christians are threatened by authorities[25] to avoid practicing their faith or face arrest and their children are denied access to education. In Iraq, Nigeria, Turkey, Yemen and other Muslim-majority countries, Christians have faced riots, beatings, arrest, and murder. And then there is Pakistan,[26] once

---

22   *Patrick Wintor, "Persecution of Chritians in the Middle East coming close to genocide," The Guardian, May 2, 2019.*

23   *Sherwood, Harriet, "Christians in Egypt face unprecedented persecution, report says," The Guardian, January 10, 2018.*

24   Chris Wilson, Ethno-religious violence in Indonesia: from soil to God." (Psychology Press, 2008)

25   *Donna Rachel Edmunds, "Iran continues to persecute Christians in violation of international law." The Jerusalem Post, January 21, 2020.*

26   *BBC News, "Why are Pakistan's Christians targeted?" British Broadcasting Corporation, October 30, 2018.*

the pluralistic country, where I happily attended school, played and celebrated with Christians. There, Christians have seen their churches blown up, have been massacred by suicide bombers while celebrating Easter, their schools burned by radical Islamist mobs, face the daily risk of being arrested for blasphemy, and their daughters being kidnapped and forcibly married to Muslims. In early 2020, a young Christian man was seized by Muslims and tortured to death after rinsing off in a well. The Muslim murderers claimed that the Christian was guilty of making their water impure.

I'm a human rights activist and have travelled to the United Nations Human Rights Council in Geneva many times over the years. Here I've met and spoken to some of the Christian victims of persecution in Muslim-majority countries. But it never ceases to astonish me how little this topic is discussed or solutions sought in the international community, especially in the West.

In 2018, I attended a conference in Ottawa hosted by the Hungarian ambassador titled "Hungarian Aid to Persecuted Christians." Maps of Muslim-majority countries featured prominently on walls but, ironically, a reformist imam, my husband and I were the only Muslims present. And amazingly, there was no mention at all of radical Islamist persecution of Christians and minorities, until my husband and I spoke up to ask why no Muslim ambassador or Muslim politician had been invited to this important event. We received no answer.

Often, authoritarian governments are helping to promote the persecution. The Muslim Brotherhood, so influential in Egypt and among radical Islamists globally, has defended robbery and extortion of Coptic Christians as justified by Islam in the "Jizya" poll tax of non-Muslims, and Muslim Brotherhood leaders stirred up violence against the Coptic Christian community after the coup in Egypt against Mohamed Morsi, the president from the Muslim Brotherhood.

As in every war and crisis, it's the women and children who suffer the most, but this is certainly especially true when it comes to Islamist persecution of Christians. In 2017, World Watch Monitor interviewed an ex-member of a network[27] that targeted Coptic women in Egypt. The man said the network began in the Seventies but has reached its highest levels in the era of current President Abdel Fattah el-Sisi. He described the process of abductions of young Christian women — frequently underage, who are typically forced into Muslim marriages — as a spider's web, in which police are sometimes involved and receive a financial reward.

The attacks on Coptic Christian women are well-planned, intentional and well-funded. The fundamentalist Salafists and Muslim Brotherhood operatives are funded by other wealthy Salafists from Gulf countries and fueled by their belief that — according to their interpretation of Sharia law — Coptic women must be forcefully converted to Islam in order to achieve salvation. Using this as their justification, they keep a lookout for Coptic women who are identifiable because they don't wear a hijab.

In some cases, Salafist men stand around in areas where Coptic Christians live and target women who are out alone. Then they either lure them or drug them and take them to secret homes where a Salafist imam and two witnesses will force them into marriage. In their own minds, the Salafists believe these vulnerable women are now their possessions and they can do whatever they want with them. Law enforcement, judges, politicians and even Al Azhar (one of the highest places of scholarship in the Muslim world now overtaken by radical Islamist ideology) are complicit in these movements because they have legitimized them. If a girl is under 18, they falsify the documents.

Due to the issue of honour, many victims' families don't report the atrocities and even if they do, they sadly know nothing will be done. I've been informed that even churches are afraid to speak out on the issue.

It is clearly the agenda of the Muslim Brotherhood and other Islamists to use religion as a tool to oppress minorities. A Pew poll published in July 2016 showed that 74%of Egyptians prefer making

---

27   *World Watch Monitor, "Egypt: Ex-kidnapper admits they get paid for every Coptic Christian girl they bring in," World Watch Monitor, September 14, 2017.*

Sharia law the official law. Ahram Online also reports that Islamists have called for cancelling the implementation of the Convention on the Elimination of all forms of Discrimination Against Women, adopted in 1979 by the UN General Assembly because, they say, "it contains articles that contradict Islamic Sharia."

The persecution of Christians in Muslim lands is not only a Christian problem. It's a Muslim problem. It is not up to Christians to save themselves. Muslims must make it stop. We can talk all we want but unless we have tangible solutions the problem will not go away. First and foremost, we Muslims must take it upon ourselves, working with our governments if need be, to create havens and refugee opportunities for Christians who are being persecuted and in danger. And we must bring our Muslim voice to put pressure on the international community to speak out against the atrocities against Christians in Egypt, and everywhere else that Islamists persecute people of faith. And we must pressure western countries to link any aid given to Muslim countries to ensuring the proper protection of minorities. Canada sends hundreds of millions[28] of dollars in aid to Egypt, Nigeria, Afghanistan, Iraq, Jordan and Pakistan — all countries where Christians still face persecution. The United States provides billions of dollars a year in aid.

We should also find ways to use lawfare to sue governments and institutions like Al Azhar. This has already been done with governments that promote terror. In 2012, the same year that the Harper government in Canada cut diplomatic ties with Iran, it also adopted the Justice for Victims of Terrorism Act,29 which allows victims to sue terrorists and those that support them, including certain foreign states, for any damages caused by terrorist acts anywhere in the world. The first case in Canada was brought against the Iranian government, which fought hard but lost the key court battle when an Ontario judge ordered the Islamic republic's non-diplomatic assets in Canada to be handed over to victims of terrorist groups sponsored by Tehran.

---

28   *"Statistical report on international assistance," Government of Canada, n.d.*

29   *"Justice for victims of terrorism act," Justice Laws Website, March 13, 2012.*

The $13-million case was the first challenge of the Justice for Victims of Terror Act. The law allows victims to collect damages from state sponsors of terror groups. Canada has designated Iran and Syria state sponsors of terrorism. If it can be done for terrorism, then why not for the persecution of Christians, many of whom have had to flee to western countries, including Canada, abandoning their homes, their businesses and so much more.

Political Islam

Political Islam is the major force shaping the Middle East region today, and a dangerous one at that. The real question is if it can be tamed, and, more pointedly, what the West can do to bring about positive change during this pivotal time in history. But first, we have to understand what we're dealing with.

Political Islam, or "Islamism" as we call this phenomenon in the West, is an armed political ideology similar to Bolshevism and Maoism. It is essentially religiosity cloaked as a movement that operates as a virulent ideology of warfare — jihad. It demands radical reorientation of Muslim societies to comply with Sharia law that repudiates modernity in all its forms, and it has brought death and devastation both within the Muslim world as well as outside its borders. In some ways, Islamism is more dangerous than outright terrorism. Terrorism can be a manifestation of Islamism. But terrorism can be identified by violence, while Islamism is fighting a war of ideas.

It is essential to note that, historically, while this aberrant thinking dates back centuries, it was espoused by marginal groups and was largely kept in check. However, there was one pivotal moment in world history when that changed. In 1926, a marginal sectarian movement inside Arabia, the Wahhabis, allied with the Saudi tribe, were able to capture power and established the Kingdom of Saudi Arabia. Saudi Arabia now serves as the bastion of Islamism. It has spawned numerous militant groups that spread its extremist political Islam ideology. It spawned Osama bin Laden.

To know where political Islam is headed next, we must look to the Arab Spring of the early 2010s, which quickly soured and became a winter of Arab discontent.

Countries that had shown promise as Arabs rose up against their oppressive governments now seem to be headed instead down a darker path. Traditional Islam is in retreat. And taking hold is the mandate of the Muslim Brotherhood, one of the most central and oldest Islamist organizations; the Brotherhood was even able to come to power in its base country, Egypt, after the revolt against strongman Hosni Mubarak, and instituted an Islamist-oriented government before being ousted by a military coup.

The youthful voices of change and reason have often been stilled in harsh ways, including through sexual violence against women.

The Muslim world is presently in an upheaval of historic proportions. As once Christendom and Europe transitioned from the pre-modern to the modern world of liberal and secular values, the painful redefinition now begins in the East. The internal struggle among Muslims will likely continue over several generations, as the Muslim world painfully makes its transition, and begins a renaissance of its own.

We Muslims in the West have important inside knowledge regarding the extent to which Wahhabi teachings generating from Saudi Arabia and Islamism have together undermined what was once a rich and tolerant culture within Islam. The West must be sure to use its friends, progressive Muslims and the State of Israel to determine a clear strategy for how to ensure that Islamism is once again kept in check. If there is one country that truly "gets it," it is Israel. The Israelis understand the powerful force of political Islam and are unafraid to call it what it is. They also have decades of experience in confronting it and dealing with it on real terms. They are a powerful ally in understanding this volatile situation.

Progressive Muslims, like myself, have tried to inform western governments about what they are up against. After 9/11, we called for recognition of the true enemy: a violent ideology that could not be fought with weapons of mass destruction. However, multiculturalism and political correctness have succeeded in keeping the West from boldly confronting the enemy, with any critique of Islamism bringing accusations of racism and Islamophobia.

This must stop.

Multiculturalism has become a cover for Islamist penetration of the West. The foe is formidable and had already infiltrated our back yard. Political Islam is on the rise in the U.K. and Europe, where some cities now have "Sharia zones," where civic law, authorities and non-Muslims are kept out, often with the government's agreement, and Islamist authorities and Islamist law rule. There are entire areas of Norway where non-Muslims are not safe.

The weeding out of Islamism and the Islamist threat lodged inside the West is the essential prerequisite — the first step — in defeating the global jihadi warfare of Islamists and in helping Islam reconcile itself with the modern values of science, democracy and human rights. To do this we must follow Israel's lead and look with clear eyes into the nature of political Islam, and confront it head-on, without fear of being called politically incorrect.

Q

Qur'an

For Muslims, the Qur'an is the word of God as revealed to the Prophet Muhammad over a period of 23 years. The literal meaning of the word Quran is "the Reading". The message was an oral message and, since Muhammad was unlettered, the words were transcribed on scraps of paper, tree bark, and animal skins. It was only after the death of the Prophet that his companions compiled the Qur'an into book form. For reasons known only to them, instead of compiling the revelations in chronological order, they assembled them in order of length, from longest verse to shortest. Therefore, trying to understand the historical and social contexts of passages in the Qur'an is a challenging task. Furthermore, in many passages, the train of thought is difficult to discern. Passages can move quickly from topics such as praising nature as created by God to thunder and lightning on the Day of Judgement.

Thomas Carlyle, on reading George Sale's English translation of the Qur'an in 1734, said that the book is a "wearisome confused jumble, crude, incondite; endless iterations, long-windedness, entanglement ... insupportable stupidity, in short!"

Having said this, there is a sublime beauty in reading and listening to the Qur'an — which is always recited in Arabic — even if one does not understand the language. The poetry and rhythm are mesmerizing. Arabic was the language of the people the Quran was revealed for; therefore, it is the original language of the book.

The Quran is not a book of laws. Rather it is a book of ethical and moral guidance. Upon reading the Quran, one realizes that it is full of stories of past Prophets, Messengers and the revelations that came before i.e. Judaism and Christianity. Its also interesting to note that the Quran surprises many non-Muslims by mentioning for example Jesus more times than Mohammad. It has a chapter called Mariam which is about the birth of Jesus and the story of his mother Mary.

There are many interpretations, so if you open copies of the Qur'an side by side, you will read slightly different understandings, which is fine until someone takes sentences out of context. Taking Qur'anic quotes out of context is a specialty of the Islamists who use cherrypicked and incomplete passages to support their radicalism, repression and violence. Historical context is also key to understanding the Qur'an, as many verses were meant for a certain time and place and are not universal. Besides, Arabic is a language in which one word can have two or more meanings, so the intent of the translation is left to the translator. Islamists have taken advantage of all this room for the Qur'an to be misconstrued, misrepresented and manipulated, to suit their own dangerous agenda.

Helping them is the fact that, for over 1,400 years, most interpretations of the Qur'an were written by men. It was only in 2007 that the first version was written by a woman, Dr. Laleh Bakhtiar. Its key difference is that in the chapter on women, where most men have translated the text to say that men can beat women lightly in case of disagreement, Dr. Bakhtiar has translated it to mean men should, as a last resort, "move away" from their wives. Translations and interpretations are only as blessed as their authors. There is also some talk about newly discovered texts and scrolls (such as the Sana'a manuscript found in 1972), but they have not been verified yet.

Both Muslim extremists and non-Muslims have quoted lines out of context to justify jihad. It's only in the past decade that there has been some critical study of the Qur'an by serious scholars. Yet those who have attempted to dig deeper into the origins of the Qur'an, like ex-Muslim Ibn Warraq, have been branded heretics by those who use the Qur'an as a political tool and want to keep it that way. The texts of other religions, however, are routinely debated, deconstructed and reinterpreted. In Judaism, the Talmud is pretty much a collection of arguments[30] about interpreting the Torah. Debate and disagreement are a healthy part of any religion, and Muslims who are comfortable in their own faith do not fear questions or differing opinions. Islamists, however, are as insecure and neurotic about the Qur'an as they are about everything else. They know that their belief in their version of the Holy Book is the one they want to be true as a way to justify their sexist, abusive and harmful beliefs. They claim their ideology is based on the Qur'an. In reality, they manipulate the Qur'an to justify their ideology.

---

30   *Tzvi Freeman, "Why can't the Rabbis agree on anything? The Jewsih obsession with arguments," Chabad.org (blog), n.d*

R

Rape Gangs

England today is living under a suffocating atmosphere of extreme political correctness regarding anything to do with Muslims. Prime Minister Boris Johnson was blamed for violence against Muslims for daring to criticize the burqa.[31] Under London Mayor Sadiq Khan's leadership no one dares speak out against Islam or Muslims. Police arrest people[32] for tweeting offensive things about Muslims.

So, to host a rally in England against atrocities committed by Pakistani men is quite a feat.

I was invited to attend the rally in August 2018 by Baroness Caroline Cox, a crossbench member of the British House of Lords and CEO of Humanitarian Aid Relief Trust, a group providing assistance for people in conflict zones or who are persecuted. She has also helped many young women who were victims of Sharia councils in Britain;

---

31   *Nazia Parveen, "Boris Johnson's burqa comments led to a surge in anti-Muslim attacks," The Guardian, September 2, 2019.*

32   *Jim Edwards, "In Britain, police arrest Twitter and Facebook users if they make anti-Muslim statements," Business Insider, May 26, 2013.*

there are estimated to be over 100 such councils operating in the U.K. And she was at the rally to show support for victims of the grooming gangs in the country.

Grooming gangs are men, Pakistani men, who have been exploiting young British girls who are homeless or in crisis, drugging them and then raping them and selling them as prostitutes. The gangs have particularly flourished in Rotherham, Oxford and Huddersfield. The girls are typically underage, as young as 11 years old.[33] The men keep them captive. Some of the girls have ended up dead.[34] Literally thousands of children are estimated[35] to have been victimized.

The event was organized by Toni Bugle, founder of Mothers Against Radical Islam and Sharia. After fleeing abuse at home, Bugle was, in her words, "pimped out by Muslims." She has since made it her mandate to support victims, expose the crimes and work towards legislation that will make it easier for abuse victims to get justice.

The situation with grooming gangs has been allowed to become so awful because of political correctness. Police and social services did not want to identify the perpetrators, because they were largely Pakistani males who operated under on the principle that "white" girls are easy prey. Sarah Champion, a Rotherham MP *had to resign* as shadow equalities minister after a controversial article published in the *Sun* newspaper, where she correctly wrote that, "Britain has a problem with British Pakistani men raping and exploiting white girls."

And so the rally had been organized to call out the abuse, without fear of being politically incorrect. It was to expose how law enforcement and the authorities have failed so many young exploited girls. And it was to highlight, also, Muslim women who have been discriminated against in their own communities through Sharia councils, something

---

33   *Brad Hunter, "Twisted UK sex grooming gang's 'campaign of rape' had victims as young as 11,"* Toronto Sun, *October 20, 2018.*

34   *Will Taylor, "Victoria Aglogia: The tragic tale of the 15-year-old girl who was abused for fun,"* Yahoo News UK, *January 14, 2020.*

35   *Lizzie Dearden, "Grooming 'epidemic' as nearly 19,000 children identified as sexual exploitation victims in England,"* The Independent, *December 28, 2019.*

Baroness Cox has been working to fight. In 2012, upon introducing her Arbitration and Mediation Services (Equality) Bill to the House of Lords, Cox said: "Equality under the law is a core value of British justice. My bill seeks to preserve that standard. Many women say: 'We came to this country to escape these practices only to find the situation is worse here'."

One speaker at the rally spoke about her daughter Becky, who was abused from age 11, trafficked, and killed at 13. The perpetrator was a Pakistani who had been selling Becky to many other men in other cities. The police called the death "an accident."

Another speaker was a young girl named Samantha, who was first raped at age 11, had a forced abortion at 12, and was then trafficked by grooming gangs for many years. This young girl trembled and wept as she told us she is under psychiatric care since she can barely get through the day.

Then we heard the story of Roma, a Muslim girl of Pakistani heritage. She had a Sharia marriage in Pakistan and when she arrived in the U.K., she became the victim of her husband's violent physical and emotional abuse. Her husband left her, taking all her money and leaving a note announcing he was divorcing her — "talaq," written three times, is considered a valid divorce by Sharia courts and is a tactic used by Muslim men to abandon their wives. And she could not get a settlement from British courts because the husband ran off to Pakistan.

Whether they were victims of the grooming gangs or victims of local Sharia councils, these women all had one thing in common: They were looking for justice from a British system that had once stood up strongly for women's rights. Now the system had become so politically correct it would not even name the perpetrators of these offences — as it might be hurtful to Muslims — let alone put an end to these crimes against women.

Religion by Force

I once participated in a multi-faith television panel discussing the question of whether young people are running away from religion. Joining me were a rabbi and a pastor. The question raised by the show's host was whether young people were being repelled by dogma and forced religiosity.

The pastor spoke about how Christian youth are not comfortable with following dogma and want the freedom to practice the faith in their own way. The rabbi agreed, adding that we are fortunate to live in a country that affords us religious freedom, which is an important component for a thriving faith community.

That isn't the case everywhere. Not in many countries, and not in many families. Too many to count.

The idea of this dialogue came after a young girl from Saudi Arabia named Rahaf Mohammed ran away from her family, her country and her faith because she said she was being forced into religiosity. At 19, she ran away from her family on a trip to Kuwait and boarded a flight to Bangkok, where she was detained by authorities in an airport hotel after her parents reported her missing: Under Saudi Arabian law, women are not allowed to travel without permission from a male. At the Bangkok airport, a Saudi representative took her passport away.

While she was in the hotel, she used social media to publicize her plight to the world and plead for help. Her father was a town governor and she said her family had denied her education, abused her, and had tried to force her into marriage. She said was in danger because she had renounced Islam and feared her family would murder her — an honour killing — if she were sent back to Saudi Arabia.

Thai officials were ordered to help the Saudis, not Rahaf, and tried forcing her from the room to deport her back to Saudi Arabia. After court filings, an apparent change of heart by the Thai authorities, and intervention by the UN High Commissioner for Refugees, she was allowed to travel to Toronto, where Canada had offered her refuge.

Her family issued a statement, publicly disowning her, calling her "unstable" and her behaviour "disgraceful and insulting."

Rahaf was fortunate to have gotten away from the Saudi kingdom and, while I am very glad she has found sanctuary in a free country, there are thousands of other women in Saudi Arabia — and many more outside Saudi Arabia — who still face religion by force.

Forced religiosity is not about God or faith. In Muslim theocracies, it is about power, patriarchy and control, and has nothing to do with spirituality. In these countries, men are the religious leaders and women are the ones who are forced to follow an ideology that dictates what they must wear, whom they can meet, where they can go and how they must practice Islam. These dictates are enforced by religious police.

And with it comes abuse. In 2020, more than a dozen women's rights activists were still imprisoned in Saudi Arabia without having had a proper trial, as reported by Amnesty International,[36] after they had been arrested more than two years earlier for peacefully advocating the right for women to drive and against the male-guardianship system, which forces women to seek permission from men to do things outside the home.

"In prison, many suffered mental and physical anguish — including torture, sexual abuse and solitary confinement," Amnesty International said. One of these women is a graduate of the University of British Columbia, Loujain Al-Hathloul.[37] She was kidnapped in the United Arab Emirates, on the order of Saudi authorities, and sent to Saudi Arabia. Her parents say she showed obvious signs of torture.

Another is Samar Badawi, the sister of Raif Badawi, the Saudi blogger sentenced to jail and flogging for "insulting Islam" and "apostasy." Raif's wife has taken refuge in Canada, and the Canadian government's call for the freeing of his sister Samar prompted the

---

36   *Amnesty International, "Saudi Arabia: 'heartbreaking' anniversary marks two-year detention of women human rights defenders, May 14, 2020.*

37   *Bhavi Mandalia, "Woman of the day: Loulain Al-Hathloul," The Pledge Times, November 11, 2020.*

Saudis to break off diplomatic ties with Canada and order a freeze on any new trade with Canada.

Meanwhile, dozens more women in Saudi Arabia, who had since been released after being arrested on similar charges, are still facing trial and punishment.

While we know that religious freedom is not the norm in Saudi Arabia, this abuse of women goes beyond religion. These are human rights violations. And we see this happening in many other Muslim-majority countries, too. In Iran, for example, women are jailed and tortured for simply uncovering their hair. After a 2019 viral protest that saw women proudly removing their headscarves on social media, many were charged with "inciting prostitution." Jail sentences handed down by the Iranian courts to these peaceful activists have ranged from 12 to 24 years[38] *each*. That's on top of the lashings they have been ordered to receive. Other women have been jailed for posting online videos of themselves dancing,[39] or for attending soccer matches.[40] They have to go disguised as men, as women are banned from all sporting events.

Interestingly, when FIFA, the world soccer federation, began putting pressure on Iran over its arrest of the women soccer fans, a funny thing happened: Iran began to relent. In 2019, it released women being held for attending FIFA matches. In October 2019, it allowed women to buy tickets and attend an early World Cup qualifier match between Iran and Cambodia. Thousands of women[41] attended.

It's not even close to achieving true freedom and equal rights, but it's a start.

---

38   *Amnesty International UK, "Iran: Activist sentenced to 24 years in prison," May 18, 2020.*

39   *Laura Italiano, "Iran continues to arrest young women for dancing videos," New York Post, November 1, 2019.*

40   *Human Rights Watch, "Iran: Women detained, accused of flouting stadium ban," August 16, 2019.*

41   *Tariq Pania, "Iran allowed women to attend a soccer game for the first time since 1981," New York Times, October 10, 2019.*

So what can the world can do? As FIFA demonstrated with its influence over the soccer ban, pressure from the right places matters. The international community should use similar tools to pressure Saudi Arabia, Iran, and other Muslim countries to clean up their human rights abuses and give women full rights and freedoms.

And it would be particularly helpful if we could count on the support from those American Muslim leaders like Linda Sarsour, Ilhan Omar and Rashida Tlaib, who claim to stand for women's rights in the U.S., but who more often sound like defenders of Islamist patriarchy abroad. I'll be waiting with bated breath.

S

Sharia

Let me give you a quick Sharia 101. Sharia is a word that means "flowing path to water": it reflects fluidity and is supposed to be totally flexible and applicable to this day and age, dealing with current issues. That, of course, is exactly the opposite of the rigid, doctrinaire way that Islamic fundamentalists apply their versions of Sharia-based rules.

Islamists see their backward and severe version of Sharia as the only acceptable way to run a government and a justice system. They have already imported it into western countries and seek to make it the law of the land in the U.S., Canada and Europe. In fact, Sharia is mentioned only three times in the Qur'an, where it used to mean moral and ethical guidance. Normal observant Muslims are able to implement Sharia into their personal lives without any side-effects, because, unlike Islamists, they are not trying to force their version of Sharia into the public sphere, and because they do not try and use Sharia as a parallel legal system in a non-Muslim environment, in opposition to their country's secular justice system. In reality, Sharia itself states that it cannot be introduced into a non-Muslim country.

That Sharia has played a pivotal role in Islamic history as a means of bringing diverse groups of Muslims within a single legal religious framework, is beyond dispute. However, I don't for a moment believe that the spread of Sharia is an intrinsic element of Islam in the life of every Muslim, certainly not as public law.

The claim made by some Muslims that Sharia is "divine" cannot be validated logically or theologically. It is derived from four sources: the Qur'an (the scripture of the Muslims); Hadith and Sunna (sayings and practices of the Prophet, not all of which are validated); Ijma' (consensus of the community); and Qiyas (analogical reasoning) or Ijtihad (independent judgment). Of these sources, the Qur'an is the only source believed by Muslims to be divine.

Over time, Sharia has stood still, without development, and has therefore started to stink. This is an inevitable outcome when water is left stagnant. Sharia has become totally manmade and at the same time it has facilitated some of the most heinous and violent phenomena.

It is used in Sharia-run Muslim countries to justify the amputation of limbs from those convicted of theft. It is used to justify stoning women accused of adultery. It is used to justify the hanging or stoning of accused homosexuals. It is used to justify whipping as a punishment for crimes.

And of course, it is used to justify honour killings, which are even legally permitted in Jordan's official penal code. I was once invited to present a paper at the UN Human Rights Commission asking the UN to table honour killings as an international criminal offence. I was up against the Organization of the Islamic Conference, almost entirely made up of Muslim men. It was perhaps the most intimidating moment of my life.

I pointed out that what is particularly shocking is that, after murdering a sister or daughter, these criminals are walking away scot-free because the Islamic law of Quisas (or retribution), allows the heirs to pardon the murderer. So a father, for example, can pardon a son who kills his sister, even if the father supported or arranged the murder.

Then, of course, we have the phenomenon of female genital mutilation (FGM). The United Nations Development Fund for Women estimates that more than 130 million girls and women alive today have undergone FGM, mainly in Africa and some Middle Eastern countries. What is more, a further two million girls a year are at risk of adding to the former statistic. FGM is being practiced among immigrant communities in Europe, North America and Australia and many governments are turning a blind eye to this epidemic because they believe it's based in Sharia.

The entire discourse in the Qur'an on women is rights-based but in Sharia, thanks to manmade secondary literature, the discourse is duty-based. In truth, the violent and misogynist Sharia that is practised today in Muslim countries is not the Sharia of the Qur'an. Sharia has been reinvented by Islamists, as Jessica Marglin, professor of religion at the University of Southern California, recently noted:

"On the contrary, this interpretation [of Sharia] is related to a particularly modern approach to Islamic law, one that is typical of Islamism. Islamism is an approach to Islam and the Sharia that arose in the 20th century across the Muslim world. Among its best-known example is the Muslim Brotherhood, which originated in Egypt and argued, for instance, that Sharia was indispensable to a vibrant Muslim community."

Marglin adds: "Today, many Islamist political parties point to a revival of the Sharia as a political solution to the problems plaguing Muslim-majority societies, including corruption and inequality."

Of course, abusing women and minorities and mutilating people and pretending it is all part of some divine legal system will not fix what is wrong with Muslim societies. Quite the opposite. I have absolutely no doubt in my mind, as a believer, that God did not create women or anyone else to be mistreated and used as second-class human beings in any faith. The spread of Sharia as an exploitative political tool is an example of how some men have misused and twisted concepts in Islam to legitimize their crimes.

Suicide Bombing

For hundreds of years and throughout the entire history of Islam, until very recently, there was no record of suicide being used as a weapon.

Yes, there are traditions of sacrifice and valour, as Muslims faced far graver threats and challenges than they are up against today. And yet history records no exemplary acts of suicidal destruction. Although suicide attacks are not exclusive to Islam (the Japanese had their kamikaze pilots in the Second World War), terrorist suicide bombing is associated strongly with Muslims because radical Islamists have used it continually since Shiite terrorists first employed it in 1983 to blow up the U.S. Marine barracks in Lebanon. Since then, thousands of terrorists have used suicide bombing to kill tens of thousands of innocent people, in Iraq, Pakistan, Afghanistan, Syria, Lebanon, Israel, Russia, Egypt, Libya and elsewhere. Including in the United States, where the 9/11 attacks constituted perhaps the most devastating suicide bombings in history.

It is unsettling that suicide bombing has become so connected to Muslims, because many Muslim clerics and scholars, well-versed in the Qur'an, remain ominously silent when it comes to condemning suicide bombers and acts of terrorism against civilians.

In fact, suicide bombings challenge two fundamental principles of Islamic ethics: the prohibitions against suicide and the deliberate killing of non-combatants. The Qur'an states clearly that killing one person is like killing all of humanity and taking your own life is a sin. Today, the Muslim world stays dangerously silent when Israelis, Americans or non-Muslims are blown up by radical Islamist terrorists. And from the same pulpits where hate is spewed, comes the potent sanction of these murderous missions. Young impressionable Muslims are led to believe that suicide missions will take them straight to paradise, with promises of a harem of virgins awaiting them (of course these decrees are normally given by males!).

These perpetrators are not practicing Islam. They are promoting a suicide cult that practices hatred and one that dehumanizes the victims of their violence — whether they are Jewish, Christian, Hindu or other Muslims — as a way of justifying their murder. If I had the power to, I'd immediately pass a fatwa declaring these cults outside the fold of Islam. It's appalling — and telling — that so many Muslim scholars, who do have that power, would rather not.

T

Totalitarianism of Thought

I was born and raised in Pakistan. Later in life, my husband and I lived in at least three Arab cities. We have also traveled extensively through most of the Muslim-majority countries. As a young couple, our goal was to establish our careers and gain financial stability.

We quickly learned that in order to achieve these goals, there were certain things we could never discuss publicly. This included absolutely no criticism of the ruling family in any Muslim country or any aspect of religion, government, laws, gender inequality or human rights aberrations — all of which we saw.

In short, there was no real freedom. This is standard in Muslim countries. Totalitarianism, particularly totalitarianism of thought, is what Islamists require in order to maintain power. There can be no questioning, no criticism. Their subjects cannot be allowed to speak freely, for fear that their subjects will like the sound of different ideas better than rule by strict and rigid Islamism.

Frighteningly, this totalitarianism of thought is also becoming standard in countries where Islamists are gaining influence.

At the end of 1988, we moved to Canada to embrace the values of freedom of speech, freedom of (or from) religion, gender equality and a healthy respect for debate and discussion. It took some time to absorb all this and feel empowered to speak out. I started by writing in the local newspaper. I was thrilled that I could finally freely critique and question the status quo — especially gender issues and the growing Islamist agenda I saw.

Can I do this in Canada today? The answer is a resounding no. Is Canada beginning to resemble the theocracies we left behind? Yes, because Canada is starting to show signs of thought totalitarianism.

The freedoms that we came here for are at stake, with the most important of all being freedom of speech. It started with a wave of political correctness, leading to Motion 103 (M-103), a federal declaration passed by the Canadian Parliament that is an official condemnation — by the state itself — of any critique of Islam or Muslims.

Then came Bill C-25 which seeks to impose "diversity" within all corporations, complete with financial penalties against organizations that do not comply with these government standards. It passed as law in 2018.

And we have minorities running to the Human Rights Commission with complaints if they did not get their coveted job, regardless of whether they were qualified or not.

Diversity has become the buzzword for Canada's quasi-judicial Human Rights Commissions. I've always held that diversity can only happen organically (without being imposed), but it seems that now it is being forced upon Canadians.

In addition, there is Bill C-16 which prohibits discrimination on the basis of gender identity and gender expression. It became law in 2017. Taken to its conclusion, it could require that all citizens must address others by their preferred pronouns and according to their gender-identity imaginations… or else. Professor Jordan Peterson received massive backlash, including a campaign to have him fired from the University of Toronto, for refusing to agree to laws enforcing the use of preferred gender pronouns, which he correctly called "compelled speech." David Solway in a piece in *American Thinker* writes, "To describe Canada as a totalitarian state-in-progress sounds like a gross and indeed absurd exaggeration. Yet many premonitory signs are present."

Islamists have no fondness for the non-binary or LGBTQ types that have been pushing for protection by this totalitarianism of thought. But this is precisely the environment the Islamists crave, where people are prohibited by law from using language or expressing ideas that the government considers to be incorrect and offensive. And those protected most by it are the radicals in the Muslim community who want to ensure that their retrograde, anti-liberal, misogynist viewpoints are safe from criticism.

They know that the fear of being called a racist or a bigot, let alone being charged with a crime for it, does not allow for any exchange of ideas. And in that fear, freedom dies.

U

Unreasonable Accommodation

Our nation's diversity is usually something Canadians are proud of. Our politicians love to talk about it, especially to other world leaders (even though, by international standards, Canada isn't ranked particularly high[42] in terms of diversity).

Still, diversity can be something to be proud of when diversity is done correctly. In Canada, and other western countries, however, it is most often playing itself out these days in the form of clashing rights, as minorities demand what they call "reasonable accommodation" in Canadian society for their specific religious practices. More often they seek "unreasonable accommodation," in that they want Canada to adapt to their strict religion, rather than seeking, as other groups have done, to find ways to adapt their faith to Canadian society.

In September 2013, at York University in Toronto, a male student asked to be excused for religious reasons from group work in which women were included. (The man's religion was never revealed).

---

42   *World Population Review, "Most diverse countries 2020," n.d.*

Sociology Professor Paul Grayson did not agree to the student's request; he said it marginalized females, who make up a majority of students at York, and was a sexist stance. The student relented and agreed to join the class. All was quiet until the university's brass weighed in. To Grayson's surprise, the dean of the Faculty of Liberal Arts and the director at York University's Centre for Human Rights said the student's request should be granted.

The case made headlines not only in Canada but internationally, where other western countries with hugely diverse populations are also struggling with the challenges of competing human rights. Two activist groups in England started a petition supporting Grayson's decision. A poll taken by some media outlets showed that 70% of Canadians supported Grayson's decision and wanted York University to take back its decision to segregate the classroom. Canadians no doubt feared the precedent this could set for other more unreasonable accommodations. If permission for gender segregation is upheld, it will open a Pandora's box for those who will undoubtedly come forward to ask for all sorts of other concessions. As he noted in his response to the decision: "Can I assume that a similar logic would apply if the group with which he did not want to interact was comprised of Blacks, Moslems (or) homosexuals?" Grayson argued that the decision about this particular case will affect the future of gender equality at universities.

In fact, in the U.K, it has reportedly become common practice to separate men and women at some lectures sponsored by Muslim groups. And in 2013, Universities UK, the representative body of universities, issued guidance endorsing gender segregation. It was forced to withdraw it after then prime minister David Cameron intervened, stating that gender segregation should not be enforced on audiences. (He noted that this did not apply to worship services.)

The fact that the guidance was withdrawn still left open the possibility of voluntary segregation. A legal notice issued later, on behalf of a female student in the U.K., stated that "gender segregation reinforces negative views specifically about women, undermines their right to participate in public life on equal terms with men and disproportionately impedes women from ethnic and religious minorities, whose rights to education and gender equality are already imperiled."

Requests for religious accommodation are already quite common in many Canadian schools. In October 2013, some schools in Ontario said students should not dress up in Hallowe'en costumes because, according to the Niagara School Board, "some families don't participate in Hallowe'en, or can't afford costumes, and are excluded."

And at the Valley Park Middle School in Toronto, where the Lord's Prayer was removed from schools many years ago, the principal allowed 400 Muslim students to pray in the lunchroom, with girls made to stand at the back. Educational institutions typically allow Muslim students to have special assigned rooms for prayer, where, if there is gender segregation, it remains within a specific group of people. Some colleges have built footbaths and special places for ablution. There has been no public dissent. Canadians, however, are now starting to ask how far religious accommodation can go before it becomes an unreasonable impingement on the freedom of others.

In a school in Ontario's Peel school district, a group of Muslim parents took a teacher and principal to court for allowing their child to sit next to and socialize with children who have same-sex parents.

Also in Ontario, the Human Rights Tribunal of Ontario fined a landlord $12,000 for supposedly discriminated against his Muslim tenants on the grounds of their faith. The landlord, John Alabai, a Nigerian immigrant who had become a Canadian citizen, had been showing their apartment to new tenants and did not remove his shoes. In fact, he had taken care to cover his shoes to ensure they were clean when he was inside the apartment.

The current federal Liberal government, taking things to an extreme, passed a bill to restore Canadian citizenship to convicted terrorists. Zakaria Amara, a convicted terrorist, serving a life sentence for his role in a plot to murder scores of Canadians, will soon get the privilege of a Canadian citizenship. Amara wanted to detonate bombs in downtown Toronto and co-ordinate shooting sprees at the CBC and the Toronto Stock Exchange. He planned to lay siege to Parliament Hill in Ottawa and carry out executions and beheadings of politicians, including the prime minister. He will now be rewarded with citizenship. Who is the government trying to please with this accommodation? The terrorist community?

This issue of unreasonable accommodation is troubling on many levels. Not even one women's group came out in support of Grayson to lobby for women's rights or to remind the nation that a decision to support segregation is a slap in the face of equality. So-called progressive groups are loath to stand up for reasonable limits on accommodation, for fear of being politically incorrect, even when those demanding unreasonable accommodation are promoting sexism, segregation, discrimination or unfair practices.

Reasonable accommodation is good when not imposed from the top down. Reasonable accommodation is the multifaith chapel at Toronto airport, which has a large section for Muslims; unreasonable accommodation is the Muslim airport employee who insists on a separate room allocated only for him or her.

Reasonable accommodation is including Muslim books in the library; unreasonable accommodation is renaming the "Three Little Pigs" story for fear of offending Muslims, who consider pigs to be unclean, as happened at one children's festival in England.[43]

Reasonable accommodation is celebrating our religious holidays with joy. Unreasonable accommodation is criticizing others who wish to say "Merry Christmas" and celebrate their culture, too.

Many of us who come from theocratic and patriarchal countries are wholly dependent on Canada's liberal, secular values of gender equality to maintain our freedom — which others are working so tirelessly to curtail.

When unreasonable accommodation leads to gender segregation and the silencing of longstanding societal traditions, it suffocates and chokes the very values that make Canada, and other countries like it, the

---

43   *"Church school renames Three Little Pigs to avoid offending Muslims," Evening Standard, March 16, 2007.*

140

great liberal, secular democracies that Muslim immigrants specifically left their own countries to find.

V

Viral Islamism

What does the coronavirus pandemic have to do with Islamism? Islamists use every opportunity to further their subversive agendas. A worldwide disease outbreak is no different. After all, people dying is not a shocking phenomenon for them.

During the coronavirus crisis, there has been a substantial and troubling rise in anti-Israel and anti-Semitic propaganda from some Muslim-majority countries. This subtle — and not-so-subtle — messaging is directed towards Muslims living in North America, Europe, the United Kingdom and New Zealand.

What is the effect of this? Just imagine 1.6 billion Muslims in quarantine. Even if you take just 30% of them, that's a huge number of people that are home, and the topics of conversations — being promoted by Islamists on social media — are the most extreme viewpoints of Islam leading to anti-Semitism, youth radicalization, abuse of spouses and conspiracy theories.

While the coronavirus will end, the fallout it will leave behind will have to be dealt with for years to come.

In Pakistan, Abdullah Haroon, a well-known, respected and educated Pakistani academic, has been used by the Islamists to create a lengthy YouTube video about where the virus came from. He claims the virus was planned, to distract the public while other weapons were being prepared, mainly to create panic and cause just enough death to make people fearful. He says Israel will control the vaccine and has told Muslim countries it will only share the patent if they recognize the Jewish State. It's part of Israel's plan to become a world power.

In Qatar, news reports claimed that Israeli soldiers are attacking treatment centres for coronavirus victims in the Palestinian areas.

Even in the U.K., Nazir Ahmed, a baron and member of the House of Lords, has suggested conspiracies about Israel and the coronavirus. In a talk he gave about "fake news," he said ominously, "don't listen to the Israeli Defense minister's explanation of coronavirus." (He also once blamed a Jewish conspiracy after he was convicted of killing someone with his car while he was texting and driving at the same time.)

It's sad that while the world is battling a virus together, with Israel among the leading innovators for a cure or a vaccine, there are people who, instead of holding China accountable for allowing this pandemic to spread to the outside world, will still find any excuse to vilify the only Jewish state in the world.

Visions of Conquest

An Islamic scholar and grand imam in Egypt was recently demoted from his senior status and banned from giving lectures or Friday sermons for daring to question the legitimacy of the concept of Islamic conquest.

As reported by *The Arab Weekly*,[44] Nashaat Zarraa contends that Islam does not call for attacking others because of their differing religious beliefs and he noted that, contrary to the intolerant viewpoint of extremists, the Qur'an actually sanctions religious freedom. This, of course, is at direct odds with the vision of extremists, which celebrates the history of Islamic conquest and promotes the concept as justification for making enemies of those of other faiths and of non-Muslim lands.

Zarraa highlighted that obvious problem with promoting the concept of Islamic conquest:

"The risk with sanctifying Islamic conquests in such an absolute way is implicitly condoning the approach by… terrorist organisations that use conquests as justification for jihad against all those who disagree with them in thought and belief, despite the fact that Islam restricts jihad to self-defence and does not justify the use of intimidation, killing and enslaving women to spread the faith," he said.

"When (the Islamic State) ISIS entered Syria and Iraq, it applied the same approach about the history of Islamic conquests," Zarraa added. "Some jurisprudence books say that, when an imam conquers a country, he has the right to kill the men and capture the women."

Rejecting extremism, Zarraa rightly argued, cannot be done "without first critiquing and revising the heritage associated with the conquests and debunking the fallacies surrounding them that have been used against humanity."

For bringing up this issue, Zarraa was subjected to a "vicious campaign" by scholars at al-Azhar, an institution considered to be the worldwide authority of Sunni Islam. Yet, Zarraa's point opens a huge question: Outside of al-Azhar, are Muslims, or non-Muslims, even allowed to bring up this issue in our day and age?

Hundreds of years ago, brutal conquest was a way of life in the world, and not just in Muslim lands. From the Byzantines to the Romans, the Crusaders and the Mongols, invasions were how ruling

---

44   *Ahmed Hafez, "Daring to criticize Islamic conquests pre-empts extremist narratives," The Arab Weekly, February 17, 2020.*

empires established power with one other. In tribal societies like Arabia, where Islam was born, barbaric tribesmen would draw a sword and attack if a camel from one village crossed over to another. It was the way things were done.

We can't change history, but we can certainly learn from it. And theoretically we have: Today, wars that are strictly for conquest — a nation seizing another land for itself — are properly seen as brutal and barbaric.

Yet, what Muslims have done over a period of 1,400 years is still glorified in their history books and sermons — even their most heinous crimes. No criticism is allowed. Only celebration and idealization. School history books in most Muslim-majority societies abound with tales of conquests, invasions and subjugation. They give these conquests a religious flavour, calling them Muslim conquests, when in fact they were conquests by power-hungry warriors.

It's true that the spread of Islam was in many cases a byproduct of these conquests. But giving it an Islamic designation conveniently frames them as holy and protects this version of history from being critiqued.

This has made it hard for westerners to even critique mass immigration by Muslims as a "conquest," when in fact, if we look what is happening in Europe, this very much *is* a conquest, even if it is a weaponless one. Masses of people have overtaken the dominant culture of Europe and imposed their own ideology on it.

Make no mistake: This conquest has been overseen by the Muslim Brotherhood, Khomeinists and Wahhabis — institutions of political Islam that want to impose Sharia law everywhere they can.

At last, some Europeans are finally realizing what is happening and are willing to do something about it. In France, President Emmanuel Macron recently launched a campaign against political Islam, outlining tougher immigration policies so that France is not seen as a "land of asylum." In the U.K., many of those who voted for Brexit did so in hopes of stemming hordes of immigrants spilling over from Europe and war-torn lands in the Middle East. Poland, the Czech Republic,

146

Slovakia, Estonia and Lithuania have all resisted the EU's attempts to settle more Muslims in their countries. And Hungarian President Victor Orban has even gone so far as to call the refugees "Muslim invaders" because those coming in, he said, were not actually "running for their lives," but had crossed several secure countries first just to get to Hungary.

Here in Canada, former prime minister Stephen Harper dared to call Islamism the greatest threat of our time, although he lost an election in part because of it. In Quebec, there is pushback against immigration, including a ban on civil servants wearing religious garb like niqabs, because Quebecers consider themselves a "distinct society" that is threatened by unchecked immigration. For that they get called bigoted. And in the U.S., President Donald Trump is accused by the media and intellectuals of being racist for wanting to restrict immigration from Muslim countries that are known to be hotbeds of radicalism.

So are we even allowed to critique conquests here in the West? Or, like Imam Zarraa, will we end up being censored and silenced if we dare to criticize the Islamist vision of conquest?

One thing is certain: Those countries that do not learn from history and choose instead to give in to these latest conquests will become their victims.

W

War on Women

Progressives and left-wingers think they're helping fight discrimination by enforcing political correctness. But by enforcing political correctness about Muslim issues, they are doing the opposite. They are protecting discriminatory fundamentalist beliefs from being properly called out and criticized. Political correctness is particularly hurting women's rights, both in the West and Muslim-majority societies. The MeToo movement isn't much help to women who aren't prominent names, or the victim of high-profile men, in the media or big business. And in western Muslim communities the debate over head-coverings has its place, but it also provides a helpful distraction from bigger issues of sexism and repression.

That women's rights have been usurped and that women have been dehumanized by fundamentalist thinking are the sad realities of today. I hear it in testimonies at the UN, where I'm accredited with the UN Human Rights Commission, and I hear in the news from my own native land of Pakistan. My journey has been to create awareness of this human crisis based on personal experience and work in the international arena.

Here is one example of how this war against women is happening even at the UN — the international body supposedly dedicated to international peace and human rights — where I have spoken out at the UN against child marriages, which are common in the Arab world. In 2013, the UN endorsed an "End Violence Against Women" platform. Ending violence against anyone, but particularly against half the population, and violence that is usually based mostly on hurting someone because of their biological sex, might seem pretty uncontroversial. But... no.

Egypt's ultraconservative Al-Gamaa Al-Islamiya faction actually condemned the platform[45] because it contains articles "violating Islamic Sharia and general morality." This is a group that actually has a political party, called the Building and Development Party, that has held seats in the Egyptian parliament and once held the governorship of Luxor. Here I am at the UN speaking against child marriages and other abuses, while an influential political organization from the largest Arab state in the world argues that such abuse against women is good for "morality."

During the Arab Spring uprising in Egypt, women were frequently sexually assaulted, often gang raped by either government troops or anti-government protestors, and several women protesters were forced by the army to undergo "virginity tests."

In Syria, another one of the world's largest Arab states, during the civil war women have been abducted by pro-regime forces to spread fear within the population and there are many reports of rape. In Libya, rape has been used as a weapon of war and the stigmatization of victims is such that they are condemned to silence. And while most of the civilized world condemns rape and works to eradicate this trauma against women, most Muslim countries make the sentencing of the perpetrator very hard. In many cases, rape victims are the ones prosecuted, and often sentenced to brutal punishments, for committing "adultery."

---

45   "*Egypt's Al-Gamaa Al-Islamiya condemns UN women's rights document,*" *Ahram Online, March 21, 2013.*

In Iraq, Hanaa Edwar, head of the charity Al-Amal ("Hope" in Arabic) said, "Iraqi women suffer marginalisation and all kinds of violence, including forced marriages, divorces and harassment, as well as restrictions on their liberty, their education, their choice of clothing, and their social life."

And in Saudi Arabia, the worst of the worst, there are simply too many abuses to list here. Saudi women can't leave the country of their own will. Those who dare to protest are often arrested and left to rot in jail. When in 2018 news reports announced that the so-called Muslim reformer, Saudi Crown Prince Mohammed bin Salman, finally "allowed" women to drive a car in his country, I laughed out loud. Women should not need permission to exercise basic rights. In the words of a Saudi journalist Dr. Khalid Alnowaiser, "Saudi women urgently need equal rights," adding "there are always men who want to control women's rights in the name of religion or otherwise."

And even in the limited forms of democracy that exist in Muslim countries, women are either denied the right to vote or face restrictions[46] from voting in Afghanistan, Pakistan, , Oman, Qatar and Egypt. While unjustly being forbidden from exercising one's fundamental right to participate in the democratic process in one's own country is a form of violence in itself, it's unfortunately not the only one that numerous women are subject to. However, being denied the right to vote is an essential one as it prevents women from participating in the making of the laws that could protect them from all other forms of violence and discrimination they experience or may experience. Female democracy activists in Muslim countries are lobbying for nothing more than the right to have a say in the politics of their country, to be emotionally and intellectually liberated and to participate in public life free from the fetters of oppression.

Some of the issues faced by them aren't new. The United Nations Development Programme has done intensive research into the status of Middle Eastern women. Statistics show the level of education among Arab women is the lowest in the Muslim world. This, in a tradition

---

46   *Georgia Aspinall, "Here are the countries where its still really difficult for women to vote," Grazia, February 6, 2018.*

where Muslims are taught that educating one woman is like educating an entire nation, and where the Prophet Mohammed explicitly obliged both males and females to dedicate themselves to seeking knowledge.

To regard any person as property to be used and controlled is an insult to God, humanity and Islam. In the early days of Islam, there were women jurists, calligraphers and poets. Even judges. Today in Egypt, they ban women from becoming judges[47] because they are considered flighty and indecisive.

One of the warning signs of fundamentalism has been identified by the international organization Women Living Under Muslim Laws as anti-women policies. Whether it's attacks on freedom of movement, rights to education and work under authoritarian and theocratic regimes, or the imposition of unjust laws— all of these are challenges that prevent women from attaining equal status and justice.

Female genital mutilation (FGM) is being practiced among immigrant communities in Europe, Canada, Australia and the U.S. Estimates from the U.S. Centers for Disease Control and Prevention indicate that at least 150,000 to 200,000 girls in the United States are at risk of being forced to undergo FGM. According to an analysis of data from the 2000 U.S. census, the number of girls and women in the United States at risk for female genital mutilation increased by 35%between 1990 and 2000. Twenty-eight states have outlawed FGM but it happens under the radar, practiced by midwives, mothers and grandmothers.

The so-called honour killing of women who are considered to have somehow "shamed" their family continues to persist at shocking rates. There are almost 1,000 honour killings in Pakistan every year — and these are just the ones that are reported. In Pakistani tribal societies, which are the majority of the country, they follow tribal law and the people are led to believe that family honour is vested in a woman since the day she is born. A woman's body, her behaviour and even her conversation is subjected to strict codes of honour and if she digresses

---

47   *"The Egyptian woman judge" Setting the bar for gender equality." Institute for African Women in Law, n.d.*

(even a simple thing like looking at or being seen talking to a man) can be construed as dishonour, subject to drawing blood.

In a study of honour killings in Egypt, 47% of women victims were killed by a relative after the woman had been raped. In Jordan and Lebanon, 70 to 75% of the perpetrators of these so-called honour killings are the women's brothers. And here is an even bigger shocker: Part of Article 340 of the Jordan Penal Code states that, "he who discovers his wife or one of his female relatives committing adultery and kills, wounds, or injures one of them, is exempted from any penalty." Jordanian women are lobbying to change this law.

Honour killings have also become common in the western world. I was invited by a Kurdish women's group to Sweden to speak to their government because honour killings were going undetected in that country. I also spoke at the UN to call for making honour killings an international criminal offence. At the UN, unfortunately, they don't give precedence to such mundane issues!

The rise in Islamic extremism contributes directly towards oppression of women. I have personally faced sexism in the Muslim community throughout my life. I was fortunate to have a feminist father who insisted on education, so I was able to carve out my own future for myself. But if I were still in Pakistan, where women are silenced if they are considered too modern or too outspoken, I would not even be free to have this conversation. Even here in Canada, Muslim men will often admonish my husband for giving me too much freedom. (His brilliant response is to tell them that I beat him. That shuts them up.)

So where does the resistance to empowering women come from? From today's self-appointed caretakers of Muslim traditionalism who feel threatened by the phenomenon that a significant number of women are now seen in public space — a space normally thought of as reserved for men only. They see emancipated Muslim women as symbols of westernization in a negative manner. The injection of feminist voices into any debate dealing with Islam and Muslims is of course seen as a challenge to male dominance. The Muslim world is a world of patriarchy. Changing that will have to come with education of both women and men.

Many Muslim women are already fighting to end the Islamist war against women.

Pakistani filmmaker and activist, and two-time Oscar winner, Sharmeen Obaid Chinoy, has made documentaries highlighting the practice of honour killing in Pakistan as well as the abhorrent practice of men throwing acid on women's faces as revenge for some perceived offence. Pakistani-born activist Malala Yousuzai and many others are doing grassroots work. But the most important aspect of our struggle is to be able to speak out, create awareness and then bring about change from within. Grassroots women's movements in Pakistan are also working in tribal areas to bring about change from within and to change the minds of men as well.

Women in Morocco brought about landmark changes to the divorce law and also succeeded in having polygamy banned. In Tunisia, women got the law changed so Muslim women can marry non-Muslim men. And in Tunis, several thousand women demonstrated outside parliament against attempts by the new Islamist-dominated government to curtail their rights.

As Tawakkol Karman, Yemeni journalist, activist and first Arab woman to win the Nobel Peace Prize said, "My dear women! you have revolted from all over the country of Yemen, Tunisia, Egypt, Libya and Syria in order to construct a dignified life and a better future. Therefore, there is no going back." Karman also points out: "One of the necessities of partnership is for women to obtain their full rights. No dignity and no liberty for a nation which oppresses women and takes away their rights."

Then there are women reformers across the western world who have opened women only mosques and are actively at work writing and speaking out against patriarchy.

Of course, speaking out comes with its own challenges. I'm the proud recipient of a fatwa, death threats, libel cases and hate mail. I'm also, according to one sincere blogger, the sixth most-hated person in the Muslim world, because of my activism in support of women's rights. If that's what makes me worth hating, then I make it my personal goal to become Number One!

X

Xenophobia

It was the fifth year of Muhammad's prophethood and his followers were being ruthlessly persecuted by his enemies. Prophet Muhammad advised a small group of Muslims to leave Mecca and take refuge in Abyssinia, where he knew the Christian king, known as the Negus, was just and fair.

The group of Muslims under the leadership of Jafar escaped in the dead of night and made their way to Abyssinia, but as soon as their departure was discovered, mercenaries were sent to find them and bring them back to face torture and imminent death.

When the Muslims reached the court of the Negus, he asked them who they were and what they knew of Christianity and Jesus. Jafar read from the Qur'an the chapter on the birth of Jesus and said that Muslims are told to revere Jesus. He said that Christians are referred to as "people of the book" in the Qur'an.

It is recorded in tradition that the Negus stepped down from his throne and, with tears in his eyes, drew a line in the sand with his staff. Then he addressed the court and said, "The difference between us is as fine as this line in the sand and we are the light of the same candle." He then gave protection to the Muslims and did not allow them to be persecuted. If it had not been for his compassion and mercy, the Muslims would have been killed and Islam would not have taken root.

Fourteen-hundred years later, in 2017, a suicide bomb and gun attack on a church in the Pakistani city of Quetta by Islamists killed nine innocent Christian worshippers and wounded dozens of others. The attack targeted Bethel Memorial Methodist Church as worshippers gathered inside to attend a Sunday midday service.

Is this how we revere Jesus and show compassion and brotherhood and sisterhood?

It was hardly the first time Christians were targeted and attacked in Pakistan. It's an ongoing tragedy, more so because the Christian community of Pakistan has always been peace-loving and benign. Despite the fact that they are treated as second-class citizens and given menial lowly jobs, they are loyal to and love the country in which they live.

There have been ongoing church attacks in Egypt, too. But here, again, Muslims forget their history. When Malik Ashtar, a companion to the Prophet's cousin, was going to Egypt as governor, the caliph and cousin of the Prophet, Imam Ali, advised him to, "Develop in your heart the feeling of love for your people and let it be the source of kindliness and blessing to them. Do not behave with them like a barbarian, and do not appropriate to yourself that which belongs to them. Remember that the citizens of the state are of two categories. They are either your brethren in religion or your brethren in humanity...."

How quickly we have forgotten the legacy of our wise leaders. Today, we are faced with mad mullahs giving fatwas prohibiting Muslims from wishing our Christian friends a merry Christmas. Why? Have these Islamists decided that they are God Almighty? Those of us who have immigrated to the West should not forget that we are living in Christian lands and enjoy all the benefits of being here. In Melbourne, Australia in 2017 an Afghan immigrant rammed his

SUV[48] into a crowd of innocent people, killing one and injuring more than a dozen others, just days before Christmas.

Today, the line that the Negus drew in the sand has become a wide gulf of misunderstanding and violence on the part of Muslims. The plight of minorities in the Middle East is compounded by various factors including societal intolerance. Many Syrian Christians are afraid to live in Muslim-dominated refugee camps run by the United Nations High Commissioner for Refugees (UNHCR), because they are targeted by Islamists there. Many are afraid to even register with the UN agency. Religious persecution and intolerance are rampant in the Middle East and many Muslim-majority countries.

Pew published data in February 2015 that highlighted religious intolerance in Muslim-majority countries. The report, titled "Latest Trends in Religious Restrictions and Hostilities,"[49] found that "social hostilities involving religion were highest across the Middle East and North Africa." Pew measured intolerance on its Social Hostilities Index, comparing regions around the globe. According to the report, the Middle East "remained well above the global median."

What Muslims should be doing is finding ways to protect and embrace our Christian brothers and sisters so that they can celebrate their faith in peace and joy. We have learned nothing from our own faith, let alone humanity, and this is why Islam continues to be under criticism. Where is the silent majority who propagate the idea that, "Islam is the religion of peace"? Instead, we have those who accuse non-Muslims of Islamophobia at every moment, while whitewashing anti-Christian (and of course anti-Semitic) language, attitudes and attacks by Islamists.

It is time Muslims realized that we will only gain respect when we give respect to others. Christmastime and Chanukah are when we can most claim to be part of this civilization, to show we can live in peace

---

48   *Colin Dwyer, "Melbourne vehicle attack suspect pleads guilty to murder," NPR, December 7, 2018.*

49   *"Latest trends in Religious Restrictions and Hostilities," Pew Research Centre, February 26, 2015*

and harmony with others of different faith. To not do so is to silently side with the barbarians who cause only mayhem and carnage.

Y

Yazidi Persecution

In 2015, our organization, the Council for Muslims Facing Tomorrow, hosted a rally at Queen's Park in Toronto to protest the massacre of Arab Christians and especially the Yazidis in the Middle East by ISIS. We had sent the event invitation to hundreds of people including churches and members of Parliament. To their credit, the previous Canadian Conservative government did send their representatives to speak and support us. There was a small turnout by Pakistani Christians, who have also been persecuted, a sizable Jewish support group, and a handful of Muslims. Churches and so-called human rights organizations did not show up.

This tells us a lot about our collective consciousness. It also raises a question of awareness. In recent times, the atrocities against minorities in Muslim-majority countries have grown. This is evident mostly in the Middle East, where the Yazidis have become a mass target for violence, rape and murder. In 2016, on a U.S. speaking tour, I asked my audiences what they knew about the plight of the Yazidis. I'm sorry to report that 99% of the audiences knew nothing. And when I informed them, they were appalled and shocked. Rightly so.

161

The Yazidis are a peace-loving and private community, an ancient people with their roots in Mesopotamia. They are few in number — perhaps a million in total — and they just want to live and let live. But that is not to be.

Lately, an estimated half-million Yazidis have been displaced in Arab lands, and they will likely never return to their ancestral homes in Syria and Iraq. Thousands of Yazidi men have been murdered and thousands of Yazidi women were taken as sex slaves by Islamists.

And this is not the first time Yazidis have been attacked. Yazidis also suffered a genocide from 1914 to 1918, when Turkey slaughtered about 350,000 Yazidis along with the Armenians — a fact that the majority of Muslims are in denial about.

So where does this place us as caring Canadians with a mandate for the international Responsibility to Protect (R2P) Doctrine? Or the Americans and Europeans, who call themselves champions of human rights? Where does this place us as human beings with a heart and conscience? In a very sad position, I'm sorry to say.

As the international human rights lawyer *Nina Shea noted in 2015*,[50] "Over the past five years of Syria's civil war, the United States has admitted a grand total of 53 Syrian Christian refugees, a lone Yazidi, and fewer than ten Druze, Baha'is, and Zoroastrians combined." If this is not shameful then I don't know what is. And how many leading U.S. politicians are even talking about this genocide?

We don't have much say in U.S. politics, but we can address this issue in Canada.

When Rona Ambrose was the interim leader of the Conservative Party opposition in 2016, she tabled a motion in Parliament calling on the House of Commons to declare that ISIS is responsible for genocide, war crimes and crimes against humanity against ethnic and religious groups, namely, but not limited to, Christians, Yazidis and Shia Muslims in Syria and Iraq.

---

50   *Nina Shea, "Christian Syrian refugees – United States won't admit non-Muslims."* Hudson Institute, *November 2, 2016.*

Since assuming power in November 2015, the Trudeau government brought into Canada 27,190 Syrian refugees of whom 15,355 are government-assisted refugees, 2,341 blended visa-office referred refugees and 9,494 privately sponsored refugees. Among the Syrian refugees, however, many had jobs and were working, but were invited to Canada to fulfil the Liberal government's election promise to admit tens of thousands of Syrians. How many Syrians, offered the chance to live in Canada, would say no? Meanwhile, the number of Yazidi cases that were processed by the Ministry of Immigration, Refugees and Citizenship were, according to testimony from senior officials, "small," totalling only nine cases.

As the *Toronto Star*'s Olivia Ward reported in 2016,[51] there were at least 15,000 Yazidis in Turkey who would qualify as refugees. More than 400,000 were still in Iraq but displaced from their homes and Canada could have followed the lead of Germany, which issued visas to 1,000 "most vulnerable" Iraqis, including the Yazidi girls and women who escaped Islamic State captivity.

Canadians need to know and understand that while Syrian refugees may be able to go back to Syria someday when things have settled down, the Yazidis have no home to go back to.

---

51   *Olivia Ward, "Forgotten Yazidis: Should Canada be doing more to help?" The IFP, February 16, 2016*

7

Zero Tolerance

For this final chapter, I want to change the subject from what Islamists do, which was the subject of previous chapters, and discuss instead what we can do — as Muslims, and non-Muslims — to stop the spread of political Islam, extremism and terror, by employing a zero-tolerance approach.

Below is a series of questions, answers and action items that we can use to fight the extremism and violence of radical Islam.

Let me start with issues that specifically relate to Muslims and what I think most Muslims really want:

1. Most Muslims want "Islamophobia" defined and acted against at the United Nations. In Canada, the House of Commons passed an anti-Islamophobia motion (M-103) in 2017. They want the world to see themselves as "victims," not aggressors. They want Islam to be understood as the "religion of peace."

2. Most of them want to be guided by Sharia law. In the West, some Muslims have already put this in action, as we see in the U.K. and Europe where they now have set up some "Sharia zones." In Texas, Sharia tribunals are being set up.

3. Most Muslims want the word "terrorism" not to be associated with Islam or Muslims.

Here are some responses to all that. They are my responses, but they can help you too, if someone wants you to answer what you would do about these things.

First of all, is political Islam really concerned about real enmity towards Muslims, or is it actually using "Islamophobia" as a political tool? The word "Islamophobia" has been defined as an irrational fear of Muslims and Islam, but is also spun as meaning bigotry and hatred against Muslims (supposedly because there is systemic racism against Muslims). If we were to take this word at face value, then the largest display of Islamophobia worldwide is in China, where we see a state-sponsored pogrom against Muslim Uyghurs, which includes rapes, forced detention and brainwashing. How often to Muslims talk about that? Do Muslims at large not read, understand or realize that a genocide is taking place under their noses? Or is Islamophobia only a term to be used for convenience — as in, if a Muslim does not get a job, it must be due to Islamophobia? Shouldn't the Organization of Islamic Cooperation (OIC), which has been pushing for international recognition of the term "Islamophobia," put its money where its mouth is and rally against this massive attack on Chinese Muslims?

And if Muslims want to see themselves as victims and not aggressors, why are the Gazans shooting rockets at innocent Israeli citizens? They may have an argument about their rights, but why are they using violence as their tool and choosing a path of aggression? In late 2019, there was a violent incident at York University in Toronto, where Jewish students were hosting a university-sanctioned event which included speakers from the Israel Defense Forces. Muslim students and left-leaning outsiders attacked the event. Who were the aggressors here?

Muslims are also not speaking out against the violence in Yemen, which is the result of a bloody turf war between Iran and Saudi Arabia. Is this because leaders of the Muslim world have sold their allegiance to either Iran or Saudi Arabia?

As for Islam being a "religion of peace," a religion is only as peaceful as its followers who practice it. There is not a single Muslim country today that does not have an axe to grind either against its neighbours, against the West, or its own people. They are not practicing peace.

And as for practicing Sharia, it is ironic that most immigrants migrating to the West are running away from oppressive regimes and Sharia-infested societies. So now they want to set up their own Sharia councils?

Finally, I agree that it would be nice if the word terrorism — defined as "the unlawful use of violence and intimidation, especially against civilians, in the pursuit of political aims" — were not associated with any one faith, cultural group or people. Yet it is obvious that there is a small group of Muslims that are the real troublemakers when it comes to spreading terror. (To understand the full picture and ideology, see the Clarion short film *By the Numbers*. This indicates the manifestation of terror in the minds of many Muslims.)

So what can Muslims and non-Muslims do to ensure we practice a zero-tolerance policy towards political Islam and its practices of false victimization, extremism, Sharia-ism and terrorism?

First, we have to **realize that radicalization and extremism does exist within Islam, and be unafraid to say so.** Whether it's an epidemic or is it a small fraction of Muslim society doesn't matter. The damage a single individual or small group of individuals can do can be on a horrific scale.

So, in my opinion, even one is too many.

How do we challenge this?

1. Identify the problem.

2. Isolate it.

3. Treat it surgically and remove it, just as a surgeon would remove a cancerous tumor from a sick patient — because radicalization is a terminal disease.

4. Have zero tolerance for any signs of radicalization or extremism.

We also need to know and be willing to say out loud **the name of the ideology we are dealing with — Islamism — and where is this ideology coming from**. There are two sources in Sunni Islam and one source in Shia Islam. Mostly, we are facing the extremism of Sunni Islam, which comes from the Muslim Brotherhood and the Salafi/Wahhabi ideology. The Shia branch of extremism is primarily driven by the Khomeinist fundamentalism out of Iran.

We also need to be unafraid to say **how these ideologies are being spread worldwide**, including into our communities in the West:

1. **Mass immigration**. Mostly from Muslim-majority nations. According to a National Security and Defence Report published in the *National Review* in 1992, 41% of new permanent residents in the United States — green-card holders — hailed from the Asia-Pacific region, the Middle East and North Africa, or sub-Saharan Africa, according to the Pew Research Center. A decade later, the percentage was 53%. Over that same period, the number of Muslim immigrants coming to the United States annually doubled, from 50,000 to approximately 100,000 each year. In 1992, only five%of Muslim immigrants came from sub-Saharan Africa; 20 years later, it was 16%. Of the 2.75 million Muslims in the United States in 2011, 1.7 million were legal permanent residents. These Muslims may or may not be extremist in nature, but very soon after their arrival they are influenced by radical mosques and Islamist groups like the Hamas-linked Council on American-Islamic Relations.

2. **Poor vetting of immigrants.** When my family and I immigrated to Canada, we had to provide police reports from every place we had lived and give context for three generations of our families. This does not happen anymore. It is understandable that refugees and immigrants from war-torn countries can't provide

such background checks. So what do we do? There needs to be a system of extensive interviews to check that immigrants understand and accept our western values. If not, either they need to learn them and embrace them as a condition of their citizenship, or they must be turned away.

3. **Failing to stand up for western values.** Most western leaders have lost the concept of western values because of what is termed as "globalism" and the concept of "open borders." This is supported by the regressive left and Islamists who are in an incestuous relationship, and is further damaged by political correctness.

4. **The negative role played by the Organization of Islamic Co-operation (OIC).** The OIC claims to represent and protect the interests of the "Muslim world" in the spirit of promoting "international peace and harmony." In reality, I have been a regular participant at the United Nations Human Rights Council, where I've seen the OIC play games that are all about blaming the West for the weaknesses of the Islamists. Israel, of course, is their main target.

5. **Islamists infiltrating western politics.** Case in point: U.S. Congresswomen Ilhan Omar and Rashida Tlaib. I don't have to explain that they are Islamists. They've made it very easy for everyone to understand that everything they're saying is from the playbook of the Muslim Brotherhood. They support the anti-Israel BDS (Boycott, Divest, Sanction) movement and, like the OIC, blame Israel for the world's many ills, when they're not blaming the U.S. They are essentially professional hatemongers and they excel in creating imaginary enemies. The irony is that they teach others how to hate, but when they are called out on their hate, they fall back on victim ideology, claiming they are being discriminated against, which is the most effective weapon used by Islamists to silence dissent

We also need **to recognize the trends the enemy is engaging in** and, again, not be afraid to say these things out loud when we see them:

You may have noticed numerous cases where media have said that the terrorists are mentally unwell, making it politically incorrect to blame Islamists for their violence and murder. This does not mean that mentally unwell people are creating the terror, as these reports would have you believe. What it means is that terrorists are focusing on mentally unstable people to do their dirty work!

Another trend that Islamists use is to use converts to commit terrorist acts, making it harder to pin on Muslims, and instead making it about some radicalized troubled youth. But who is converting these troubled youths and radicalizing them? That's where law enforcement really needs to focus. One thing law enforcement must do is build trust with real, grassroots Muslims, not just by reaching out to official Muslim leaders, but getting to the community at every level: Women, youth, and those on the fringe.

We also must **recognize that it is the very freedoms and religious tolerance that we cherish in the West that the extremist elements think they can exploit to get away with their radicalization efforts**. We must not ever lose those important western values — for us to do so is precisely the Islamists' goal — but we must practice them in ways that do not prevent us from refusing to tolerate unacceptable behaviour from Muslims just because they are Muslims. Let us not tolerate gender-based abuse in the Muslim community. Let us not tolerate racism, anti-Semitism, bigotry and xenophobia in the Muslim community. Let us not tolerate Sharia law replacing our secular law in the Muslim community. Let us not tolerate the defence of murder, rape, genocide and other forms of violence in the Muslim community. Let us not tolerate hate speech in the Muslim community. Let us name those who do these things, and shame them for it.

And, most importantly, let us keep our free, fair and tolerant society healthy by showing zero tolerance for the sickness of Islamic extremism.

Raheel Raza Bio

Raheel Raza is president of the Council for Muslims Facing Tomorrow, a founding member of the Muslim Reform Movement, a director of Forum for Learning, an award-winning journalist, a public speaker and an advocate for human rights, interfaith dialogue, gender equality and dignity in diversity.

VISION AND GOALS:

- **EXPOSE** the dangers of a radical Islamist ideology and take back the faith.

- **EMPOWER** women to demand their human rights and pursue gender equality.

- **EDUCATE** youth about the dangers of radicalization and terrorism.

MEDIA:

- Raheel has appeared in print, on TV and on radio numerous times including CNN, Real Time with Bill Maher, BBC, CBC, CTV, TVO and Fox News.

- In 2018 she gave over 350 interviews internationally and published over a dozen op-eds.

- WTN (Women's Television Network) featured Raheel in their special documentary series titled Family Dance.

AWARDS:

- Recipient of the Museum of Tolerance Medal of Valor, 2018.

- Recipient of Canada's sesquicentennial commemorative medal for "exceptional contributions to Canada."

- Recipient of the Queen Elizabeth II Diamond Jubilee Medal for service to Canada.

- City of Toronto's Constance Hamilton award.

- Recipient of the Urban Hero award.

- Participant in the award-winning documentary Honor Diaries.

- First Pakistani woman to be included in Canada Heirloom Series titled Millennium.

SPEAKING ENGAGEMENTS:

- Universities across the U.S., including Harvard, Columbia and Brandeis universities.

- Oxford and Cambridge universities in the U.K.

- Parliaments of Sweden, the U.K., Israel and on Capitol Hill in Washington, D.C.

- TEDx Amsterdam.

- School boards and places of worship.

- The Israeli Presidential Conference in Jerusalem.

HUMAN RIGHTS:

- In her pursuit for human rights, Raheel is accredited with the United Nations Human Rights Council in Geneva and the UN in New York.

ACHIEVEMENTS:

- Gave testimony to the U.S. Congress on the topic of combating homegrown terrorism, in 2017.

- Taught courses on various aspects of Islam at George Brown College and Ryerson University in Toronto for the past five years

- Maker of a documentary film called Whose Sharia is it Anyway?, dealing with the Sharia debate in Ontario, Canada.

- Testified before the Canadian Parliament on Bill S-7, which became the Zero Tolerance of Barbaric Cultural Practices Act.

BOARDS:

- Advisory Board of The Clarion Project.

- Chairman, Advisory Board of Rebel News.

- Executive Advisory Board of the Mackenzie Institute.

- Advisory Board of the ACTV Foundation (The Alliance of Canadian Terror Victims).

- Munk Senior Fellow with the *Macdonald-Laurier Institute.*

- Board member for Creative Cultural Communications.

- Steering Committee of Parliament of World Religions.

- Advisory Board of Women's Voices Now

PUBLICATIONS:

- *Their Jihad — Not my Jihad* (Basileia Books, 2005).

- *How Can you Possibly be a Muslim Feminist?* (Possibly Books, 2014).

- *Paper: The Rise of Islamic Extremism in Canada* (Mackenzie Institute, 2013).

- *Journeys of a Spiritual Activist* (Possibly Books, 2017).

www.raheelraza.com

www.muslimsfacingtomorrow.com

http://muslimreformmovement.org

Contact: *info@raheelraza.com*

Manufactured by Amazon.ca
Bolton, ON